# Financial Ninja

*How to Practically Manage Your Finances in an Impractical World*

---

Jason Evans

Copyright © 2018 by Jason T. Evans
ISBN: 9781790530649
Independently Published

All rights reserved

No part of this book may be reproduced, or stored in a retrieval system, or transmitted in any form or by any means, including: electronic, mechanical, photocopying, recording, or otherwise without the express written permission of the author.

Cover design by Maria Esther Ruiz Arevalo

**Contents**

    CHAPTER 1—ME ................................................................................ 1
    CHAPTER 2—DEBT ........................................................................... 8
    CHAPTER 3—PAYING OFF DEBTS OTHER WAYS ......................... 32
    CHAPTER 4—RETIREMENT ........................................................... 63
    CHAPTER 5—BUDGETING AND SAVING ..................................... 92
    CHAPTER 6—COLLEGE SAVINGS ................................................ 104
    CHAPTER 7—FINAL THOUGHTS .................................................. 114

## CHAPTER 1—ME

    Why am I giving financial advice and what makes me qualified to do so are probably your first questions. Well, frankly, I am no one. I am you; I have just learned over many years and many, many failures how finally to navigate the financial waters of life. While I am not a certified financial planner, I do have a solid finance background, but these days who doesn't? I don't write for the *Wall Street Journal* and I am not the CEO of a Fortune 500 company, but the reason I think you should listen to me is the very fact that I am like you. I like simple explanations for complicated things, I like a financial plan I can live with, I like seeing the numbers laid out so that I can decide for myself, and I am not here to amass a great deal of wealth in the form of commission from you while I manage your money. I believe it is possible for you to manage your own money. I simply want, you, me, and everyone else to be able to live a life that affords us the ability to do most of the things we want to do. I want you to live a little above your means, but not suffer for it. What I will impart to you is not necessarily conventional wisdom, and probably your financial advisor, if you have one, will disagree with much of what I say, but conventional financial advisors work on commission—I don't. What is in their best interest isn't necessarily in your best interest. Your parents probably will tell you something different from what I am telling you as well. My parents, though, did neither.

    I grew up poor, not so poor that I didn't eat decently, but poor enough to have the United States Department of Housing and Urban Development (HUD) come and take what I thought was *our* house away from us. I am not saying I am scarred for life from that experience. It was an interesting experience, yet not one I would recommend you try for yourself. My parents bought the house, and I know I am dating myself here, but they bought the house for a little over $50,000 in the 1980's. The payments were around $600 a month and ultimately they couldn't make those payments. This house was no *Architectural Digest*-featured home either, but a very modest 900-square-feet-of-living-space rambler. It wasn't built to stand the test of time either. It was constructed very poorly and with, even at the time, the cheapest materials possible. If you didn't know this already, poor construction leads to moisture, and moisture leads to mold and rot. I think we could have developed our own penicillin with the amount of mold we had growing in that house. My brother and I shared a room with a bunkbed. I, fortunately, slept on the top, but the mold arched up the wall sufficiently high enough to reach my head height. Now looking back this may be why my brother, who was relegated to the bottom bunk, suffered fewer bacterial infections, but will probably suffer greater lung ailments since he ingested so many mold spores. Probably on the order of about every five months my brother and I would move the bed and then scrub the wall with pure *Clorox* bleach to kill the mold as best we could. Yearly we would have to repaint the wall, which appeared to have a direct connection to the outside wall, and like a chameleon would adopt the temperature of the surrounding environment. What lurked behind that wall could only be a forest of yearly mold rings that developed over the course of our time in that home instead, of course, of the usual insulation.

The interesting thing about HUD commandeering your home is that they were pioneer house flippers like the one sees on HGTV now. They came in and fixed our leaky roof, replaced all the drafty windows, and at least attempted to repair much of the structural failures of the house. When they had finished their work, we were treated, albeit only briefly, to a house worthy of being called a home. Then they told us we couldn't stay in that home anymore. I happened to be in my old hometown for a class reunion years later and visited this house fully expecting it to be razed and a nice new house in its place, but much to my chagrin it was in fact still standing. It turns out a family was actually living in this house, too. They were kind enough, after some cajoling, to let me, a perfect stranger, back into what was now their problem house to look around. Unfortunately, they hadn't changed it much, and after some reminiscing, mostly on my part, as these new inhabitants looked upon me like an alien, I asked them what they paid for the house. To my absolute shock they told me that had bought the house for $250,000. I immediately felt bad for this family, because that piece-of-crap house wasn't worth the $50,000 my parents couldn't pay for it.

I believe my parents' failure was most acute in regard to money management. At one point, my father made a decent salary for the 1980s, but he had a penchant for unnecessary purchases and both drank and smoked to the level of a fetish. One doesn't realize how quickly these two luxuries, if they can be called that, erode one's wealth. Even back then cigarettes were relatively expensive, and at two packs a day he quickly burned through—while throwing his butts everywhere—his net take home pay. My first bit of anecdotal advice to you is, if you are having financial difficulties and you smoke, quit or smoke a whole lot more. If you quit, you will help yourself find solid financial footing; if you want to go the other route and smoke a whole lot more, then your problems will likely be solved as well, since you won't have things like retirement to worry about.

When my father was laid off, which still happens today, we had no security funds, no savings, no equity, and no family support to fall back on, so we quickly spiraled out of financial control. I don't tell you this to garner your sympathy, only to demonstrate that financial security is an ethereal concept. We all pitched in as best we could. My brothers and I got paper routes, which, back then, were considered acceptable forms of child labor. A paper route is something that no longer exists today or, at least, it has shifted to a more institutional level. My paper route taught me all sorts of things about business and people. Unfortunately, none of it was either useful or good. You were required to manage your own paper consumption, as I quickly found out when the bill for the papers I had delivered—or in this case dumped in a field—came, and for which I had no corresponding customers. This quickly drove my little cottage industry into the ground and I realized I needed to come up with a creative way to get my business back into the black. A method presented itself in an unlikely form. I had to go and solicit residents, adults, on my route each month to ask them to pay their paper delivery bill. This is something today that would be looked upon as lunacy, since you were sending your child to all manner of strangers' houses. Today you can plot the exact location of all the child sex offenders to help your children avoid such areas. Back then I was probably collecting payment on a monthly basis from pedophiles with several victims likely writhing in pain in their basements. Since I was already in the hole I thought it made sense to try and convince these folks that paying their bill several months in advance would keep me off their porch each month to collect dues. (In retrospect, this may have been counter to their nefarious plans to also keep me in the basement.) This, for a time, allowed me to pay the supply costs of my paper route while still allowing me to fritter away any profits I had on candy and arcade video games. Also, fortunately for me, most people didn't keep very clear records of exactly how many months they had paid in advance, so when I showed up three months later—when they had already paid six months in advance—they were largely complicit in my money-making scheme. Incidentally, even operated legitimately, a paper route is a small-profit business. They try to convince you otherwise, but none of the labor and supply costs you end up carrying, like a bike, were considered in the net present-value calculations. This left literally pennies for you and millions for publishers like Mr. Hearst or Mr. Bloomberg. Added to this was my dad's need for smokes, which he satisfied with the change from our paper routes. It became clear to us very quickly that my father's desire for us to endanger ourselves in this low-profit business was motivated by the small amount of change we had on hand that he absconded with to buy seemingly, at least when compared to food, needless cigarettes. I learned a lot more than the news from my paper route that is for certain.

Things didn't improve much when I was on my own away at college. I was, like many of our children today, a victim of predators handing out credit cards to unsuspecting students as we left with our textbooks from the bookstore. For someone who was poor to have imaginary money that could be traded for goods and services was both foreign and exciting. I began abusing these magical cards almost as soon as I got them, and when I ultimately found myself in trouble with debt I sought "credit counseling". I know now this help wasn't really helpful at all. They told me I needed to cut my spending and just wait out the period of time during which I had bad credit, because ultimately I would pay off these things and then I would be able to enjoy a debt-free lifestyle. The only problem was that when I gained the skills I have now and laid out the payment schedule along with the interest payments, I wasn't going to enjoy this debt-free lifestyle until I was in my mid-forties. I got educated and slowly started taking the view the credit companies have and viewed my debt more like leverage and viewed my execution of that debt as a business. This is no different from what they did with respect to the collection of my debt. Once I gained a thorough understanding of how the industry worked, I started to use it to my advantage. That is why I think I can help you do the same thing. I don't want to lecture you on the ills of debt or the moral goodness in paying off your debt. I simply want to help you find a path to live the life you want to live now, not in your mid-forties or later. I believe if you follow even a modest number of the techniques I will teach you, you can cut the period of time to pay off your debt considerably, and in many cases without paying a lot of extra interest. You will learn how to navigate the financial waters we all find ourselves in, and in a more adroit fashion. You will be able to use debt to your advantage to have many of the things you want now, not later. You will make mistakes like I did, but I don't want those mistakes to debilitate your ability to have a fruitful retirement or for you to suffer the stress of collection agencies calling at all hours. I want to help you get out of debt and stay out of debt without resorting to extreme measures either in your spending or through the utilization of bankruptcy. I want you to be a ninja, just with finances.

Why do I want you to be a ninja? The answer is because of the unorthodox methods used by this elite group of feudal Japanese warriors. Beginning to operate in and around Japan and China in the early 12$^{th}$ century, these warriors possessed unique skills in areas that modern warriors have only begun to pursue. They were not only nimble and adroit physical fighters, but they understood those things necessary to truly win battles: better weapons, sabotage, tactical assassinations, hiding in the shadows, and the ability to penetrate protected fortresses, to name a few. Their ranks were also filled with people from atypical backgrounds, including arsonists and other subversive elements both within and external to proper society. Once in the organization, though, they fought with a ridged code and ethics. They developed weapons and protective armor that would still be formidable on today's battlefield. They were trained to be highly effective fighting forces, and that is precisely what I am hoping to teach you. I want you to become a financial ninja and to utilize analogous financial tricks to ensure that your financial goals are attained and you are protected from other would-be financial assassins.

## CHAPTER 2—DEBT

*The 1980s was an eventful period of time for the world both politically and financially. The early part of the decade was mired in a recession not seen since the Great Depression. The period of contraction was lost on my father, who didn't understand debts or finances and thought it would be a terribly good idea if he purchased, for his budding, but largely unused workshop, a metalworking lathe. Perhaps you are familiar with woodworking lathes as these are the tools that form the spindled legs of many of the chairs you sit upon to eat your meals. How they work is one suspends a dowel of wood within the lathe and when you turn it on the dowel spins. You then take a chisel and apply pressure to the dowel at various points and, voilà, a chair leg is born. Do this four more times and you can make a chair upon which to rest after a long day of wood carving. This could have been a useful tool had my father been interested in opening up a furniture factory, but he wasn't. Even more so, he wasn't about to open up a furniture factory making metal furniture, so why he would spend a relatively large amount of money, at least as compared to what he took home as pay is beyond me. A metalworking lathe is a serious tool, certainly more so than a woodworking lathe. It requires special chisels and the danger factor is raised by about ten since the little metal shavings that come off could go anywhere: your eye, your hair and then later your eye, your mouth and then your esophagus, or any number of places you wouldn't want tiny sharp metal shavings. We asked him what he intended to do with this lathe, but were given cagey and circumspect answers. None of the standard tools seemed good enough for him. Instead of a drill he got a concrete hammer drill, and not one of the versatile ones you can get today for which you can suspend the hammer feature and get a regular drill out of it, but a drill whose sole purpose was to drill through rock. Back then financeable purchases were not as prevalent as they are today either, so instead of buying on credit, he took money that could have been more wisely used on essentials like food and the mortgage and redirected them to tools and heavy machinery better suited to a construction firm. Even years later when my mother finally divorced my father and we were moving these heavy tools out of the house we asked him what he ever intended to do with these tools, but still nothing spewing forth from his heavily bearded mouth seemed to justify such purchases.*

According to the U.S. Census Bureau and their 2013 census, we all have been paying down our debts, however the level of unsecured debts has remained fairly steady. Debts are bad and I realize every financial analyst and planner will tell you that getting rid of debt should be your number one priority, and while I don't disagree with any of this, my view is a bit more liberal. I believe debt is a necessary evil that one must only manage properly to be able to still achieve the things we want but for which we are not willing to wait. Carrying a lot of unsecured debt and even some secured debts can drag down your cash flow, or the amount of disposable income you have to go out to eat or buy a Grande coffee as opposed to a Tall. The part of debt I don't like is the interest you pay on that debt. Businesses use and carry debt, though. They invest in equipment all the time, and while their debt is called leverage it is the means by which they grow their business. It is how they get more, but the bank gives them better terms than you are able to get. It is this hidden loss of income that I want to help you attack. Arguably credit holders take more than they should, but if you understand how they do it and what their motivation is I believe you can use it like leverage and grow your own home finances. First, though, let us look at how your credit score, one of the facets of this whole debt issue, and one that is probably more closely related to you than your significant other, is determined and used.

Please, if you would, indulge me if you already know some of this, but hopefully contained in this discussion of your credit score will be some useful information, because this number and file is about as unique as your fingerprint. As you may already be aware, there are currently three credit agencies, Equifax, Trans Union, and Experian, that maintain separate files on you. Why three, I don't know, but they all contain very similar information so in order to remain relevant they find different ways of displaying that information. There is now a new company on the block as well, the *Fair Isaac Co.* or what you probably know as FICO. They are not a credit reporting agency themselves, rather they provide mashups of the information offered by the other three. The company offers what they term "predictive analytics," which are supposed to determine your credit worthiness or the risk associated with you being extended credit. This FICO score is generated from the files maintained by the aforementioned three credit reporting agencies so, as I mentioned, Fair Isaac Co. is not a credit reporting agency itself, just an aggregator of available data. The credit reporting agencies and FICO all also maintain relationships, or try to, with different financial institutions. One bank may use Equifax to get their credit report on you and another may use Experian, and now that FICO has become an element of your credit pantheon, you could see the credit grantor using them as well. The files these agencies maintain are their very livelihood, so I suspect they protect that data not unlike the data was protected in Mission: Impossible-Rouge Nation—in an underwater vault. This robust canon of data stays with you, and I can only imagine others would like to get their hands on it. It turns out that with the recent breach of Equifax the data these agencies store is not as robust as we would hope, which only means keeping it as accurate as possible should be an even greater priority. Perhaps you have had to authenticate your identity before. It is this data they call upon to help identify you. Whoever is determining your identity has access to a bank of questions derived from information in these files that take the form of multiple-choice questions having corresponding answers contained in these files. The agency has a vested interest in maintaining both the accuracy of that data and its security, but hackers are becoming more and more brazen each day. I use the word accuracy in loose terms though, because—make no mistake—the credit agencies don't work for you, they work for banks and other financial institutions relying on this data to carry out their business, not yours. Yes, the agency gets a little money from you when you pay the $8 to receive your yearly credit report, if you even do that, but that is pocket change compared to what the financial institutions pay for the contracts they maintain with these companies. Once you get a Social Security card and start doing financial transactions you will have a file. Any financial transaction will begin the file and then that file will be open for a period of time exceeding your lifespan. In other words, even well after you are not around to do any more financial transactions.

The information contained in these files is only as accurate as the financial institution's reported information to them. It can become inaccurate when you get into financial difficulties, like late payments, or you start disputing charges, or someone steals your identity, or they may simply contain incorrect information, and there are many more reasons for possible inaccuracies. If you dispute a charge and get it cleared up with the financial institution, that institution is not always as diligent as you in reflecting that information to the credit agency. Another possibility is the financial institution wishing to do you some harm will report you late even though you may have been right on time or had worked out a payment schedule with the institution so that your payment could be late. Also, it could be the fault of it simply being reported by one department while the department you spoke with about the late payments is another. Banks are big and they want to make money. They have many layers of bureaucracy, and ensuring your information is accurate is not their top priority. Once something gets on that credit report, as anyone who has moved and forgot to pay their last electric bill can attest, it is hard to remove information. That electric bill could follow you for several moves after and could be the reason that you were denied the car loan you are currently apply for two years later. The agency claims to be only maintaining accurate records, but had anyone in that bill chain just informed you that you had a bill that was becoming first 30 days past due, then 60, then 90 and worse as time went by, most people would have probably cleared it up. The credit agency doesn't care what your score is, or if you can get credit, they are just concerned with how accurately the information is being reflected in your file. This is why it is incumbent on you to ensure not only that the information is accurate, but that the things you believe to be true are in fact being reflected in your file. Also, since this information feeds the FICO score, it is a good idea to ensure its accuracy as well.

    Fortunately, it has become much easier to monitor your own credit file. Most credit cards offered by banks come with free-ish credit monitoring, as well as a listing of your FICO score, often for free as well. This FICO score, though, is only for credit products that the bank offers, since they offer different types of analytical evaluations to financial institutions. The one good thing about your FICO score is that it is fairly consistent. The credit agencies have scoring as well, but it may differ from that of the FICO score and it may differ depending on which agency is reporting it. I once pulled my credit report from all three agencies and saw a range of scores that varied by about

50 points, even though they were all using the same overall range of scores. This is not an insignificant amount considering the break point for good and decent credit is about at the bend of 700 points. The credit agencies, and FICO, too, since it wants to stay relevant, all have a range from about 300 to 850. Your score within this scale can mean the difference between two candidates for a job, as well as the terms you may get on a variety of loans.

What I want to help you do in the aggregate is get these scores, all of them, higher, and explain why periods where they are not high is not something to worry excessively about. In order to do some of the things I suggest, you may see your credit scores fluctuate, sometimes significantly, but that is ok. All you really want is the best score you can get at the time you are looking to buy something with credit or are soon going to be under the terms of a loan. How sensitive these scores are to changes in your debt-to-income level, income, the rate at which you pay down the debt, and other factors is debatable. What I can tell you is negative information seems to be reflected very rapidly, whereas positive things take a little longer. As long as you don't get into significant issues like very late payments and defaults, most everything you do to pay down these debts will positively affect the scores of all of the credit agencies as well as improve your FICO score. If a debt is paid off completely with either a windfall or some of the methods I outline below, it takes about 60 days for your score to jump up in response to this satisfaction of the loan. It will jump, too, if you can pay it off or bury that debt in something that the credit agencies do not monitor, and then you will find yourself in a much more advantageous position when you are applying for new credit. We will get into all of this in due time, though, rest assured. Frankly, once you have the things you need on Maslow's hierarchy of needs, a low score doesn't affect you significantly. Once you make the big purchases in your life, like a car, a home, and a couple of credit cards for vacations, then monitoring these scores is not nearly as important, other than to prevent thieves who might be looking to steal your identity to make themselves marginally richer at your expense. I will address the impact to your credit scores as it is germane while paying debt or purchasing things. Before we do that, let us address how you should get credit, because just like with many other things, there is a right way and a wrong way to going about establishing credit

Credit seems easy to establish, and as your mailbox can attest, there is no shortage of banks and other institutions looking to extend you credit. When I went on the first day of college to get my books from the university bookstore, I was greeted with offers from various lenders right outside the store. It seemed unfathomable at that time and at my position in life, with no job and just beginning to embark on a college education, that someone would offer me a credit card. Something with which I could purchase items while not really having to pay for them right away was attractive. I seized the opportunity and soon found myself in some serious debt trouble, but I should not have leapt upon these offers, and neither should you. The rates they were offering me should have been just as unfathomable. While I disagree with these predatory practices, particularly on young adults, it exists, and just like most things that are valuable or worthwhile, good credit cards are not so easy to find. So how should you establish credit? First, you should shop for a card just like you shop for anything else that matters to you. Frankly, the jeans you purchase and love will probably wear out long before your credit card does, and those jeans won't prevent you from getting a job later, but your credit could. Take time to investigate what the bank is offering. Pay particular attention to these three things: how much are they offering, at what interest rate, and lastly, the perks of the card. I say the perks of the card are the last consideration, because those perks represent the least value. It may seem interesting that the card offers you travel points or "rewards" that can be applied to various things or even that it pays you back. In order for any of these things to happen, you have to buy a lot of items and make the bank a lot of money first. They are not going to offer you anything before they make money off of you first. If you have the time look at how much you have to purchase to get free miles on a travel card, for example, you would be amazed. You could likely buy several round-the-world trips on your own if you just bought them outright. By the time you make all those purchases you will not want to travel anymore or you will have retired and wish only to tend to a small house and garden. Don't get me wrong, there are ways to take advantage of these deals. If you travel a lot for work and can apply these purchases to your personal card then it is worth it, or if you can gain points by purchasing things you would be purchasing anyway, and you pay off the card, then they may be very much worth it. For most of us the perks are really just the ability to purchase things we can't currently afford outright, but which we could afford if we paid for them over time. Don't be misled by card offers through retail stores, either. These cards are backed by a bank or some such financial institution also subject to profit-driven concerns. Furniture stores are very happy to let you purchase a whole living room set for $10,000, and then charge you as much as 26% or in some cases even higher to pay off that large purchase. There are plenty of people along that chain that need to take some of the money you will be paying monthly and this drives up the interest rate. This will only make the purchase of the furniture you entertain your guests upon even more expensive. Financial intuitions that are not banks do not have the cash reserves to be able to offer a great amount of loans to customers, which in turn would allow them to offer these loans at lower rates. Think of it like bulk shopping. Banks offer more at less as opposed to these other financial institutions that offer less and in order to make any money must increase the rate. So, if you want my advice, stay away from these kinds of card offers. There are some notable exceptions. *Barclays*, for example, backs an *Apple* card that often allows you to buy an *Apple* product and pay it back *interest free* over various periods of time depending on the amount of the purchase. Also, some stores offer debit-style cards that really are just linked to your checking account, but which still accrue points that you can build and use for future purchases. These are also fine as long as you have the money in your checking account, because then the rewards can be utilized without building you a pile of debt right next to the rewards. Cards that offer introductory or periods of low or no interest are powerful tools also, but make sure you intend to pay them off or to transfer that balance by the expiration of that introductory period. Short of these few exceptions you should look primarily for a decent line of credit coupled with a decently low interest rate.

Your first card is not going to have a very high credit limit, but I will explain later some techniques you can use to get it higher. The interest rate will not be all that good either, but even starting out, a rate much higher than 14% is pushing my level of acceptance, and it should be pushing yours, too. There is far too much competition to accept very high interest rates these days. The bank has lots and lots of actuarial tables that indicate your credit worthiness, so there is not much use in trying to convince them that you are better than what their tables tell them, and why you deserve special treatment. I cannot tell you exactly what to accept, but a credit line of something between $1000 and $2000 and an interest rate lower than 14% is a good enough start to your financial adventures. Once you get the card the first question is, what should you do with it? Well, in order to make it work for you, you must use it. Most people will tell you that you should pay off your balance each month and not run up the card to the very limit of its credit. I agree you shouldn't run up the card, but if you expect to be granted a higher limit you must play the game the bank wants you to play—to an extent. Just like when you gamble at a casino hoping to get perks like a free hotel room or free dinner, you must lose a little before they will give you these perks. You have to be making money for the bank for them to grant you more credit or better interest rates. Make no mistake, though, the bank is making money on you no matter what you do. That balance you paid off still made them money in the month they had it because they exploited things like arbitrage and other methods available to large financial institution but which you cannot participate in. For them to extend you more credit you must use the card and let it carry a balance that charges you some interest. Again, I am not suggesting that you go out and max the card hoping that the financial institution will then turn around and offer you a better rate or extend you more credit, because they won't, not right away at least. I am suggesting using it for nominal purchases, things you would buy anyway, like groceries, and paying off the balance, but not right away. That way you are giving the bank its extra money and in turn they will, more rapidly, at least, extend you more credit. This won't happen immediately, as I said. Most banks look at the activity on the card over the previous six months and then they may or may not extend you more credit. Getting better interest rates takes even longer. Sometimes they will let you know you are eligible for more credit and sometimes some banks will not say anything. You, too, can ask them about every six months to look at your ratings and to let you know if you are eligible for more credit, but use that card wisely and, mark my words, they will extend you more credit. Again, they do this not because they are nefarious, but because extending you more credit means potentially more money for them. Higher balances lead to higher amounts of money, on either a fixed interest rate or even one slightly lower. After all, 14% of $5000 is more than 14% of $1000.

Some of the limits placed on the cards credit limit will be related to your income, of course. Unfortunately I can't help you change that, at least, not easily. As your income rises though, expect to be extended more and more credit. If you follow my advice and manage the credit you are offered wisely you will be able to live at means higher than whatever income you find yourself earning.

How many cards should you carry or use? Current wisdom is to carry two credit cards, but it is likely you may have a few more than that if you have any of the store cards or, like I do for *Apple* products. This is a card I use just for the purchase of new phones or computers. The key to my system though is to have two solidly operating cards, possibly three, with interest rates as low as you can get and a comparably decent credit limit. If you are reading to this point I am assuming you probably did not do any of these things and didn't manage your credit quite as wisely as you could have, but do not despair. That is the real topic of this chapter. I want to help you clean up that credit without credit counseling, or bankruptcy, or anything else that has long term effects on your credit and your life.

Not all banking credit cards are created exactly equal either. Credit unions generally offer better rates and have better benefit offers than do commercial banks, but not everyone is eligible to be a member of these credit unions. The two largest credit unions United States Automobile Association (USAA) and Navy Federal Credit Union (NFCU) are excellent credit unions, and membership can often be acquired through either a family member, friend, or partner even if you didn't serve in the military. If you can get membership to either of these or perhaps a credit union associated with your place of work like a university or large company then I would highly recommend your two cards, or at least one, come from institutions like these. As a union the financial institution can offer you better rates because members share, sometimes directly, in the overall financial wellbeing of the bank. This generally translates into better care being given to you and your money. Why it is so bad that you got into a situation requiring some more advanced financial maneuvers and how we are going to get you out of a less than exemplary financial status is what I want to explore next.

Some of the limits placed on the card's credit limit will be related to your income, of course. Unfortunately, I can't help you change that, at least not easily. As your income rises, though, expect to be extended more and more credit. If you follow my advice and manage the credit you are offered wisely, you will be able to live at means higher than whatever income you may be earning.

How many cards should you carry or use? Current wisdom is to carry two credit cards, but it is likely you may have a few more than that if you have any of the store cards or, if you have a card for *Apple* products, as I do. This is a card I use just to purchase new phones or computers. The key to my system, though, is to have two solidly operating cards, possibly three, with interest rates as low as you can get and a comparably decent credit limit. If you are reading to this point, I am assuming you probably did not do any of these things and you didn't manage your credit quite as wisely as you could have, but do not despair. That is the real topic of this chapter. I want to help you clean up that credit without the need for credit counseling, or bankruptcy, or anything else that has long term effects on your credit and your life.

Not all banking credit cards are created exactly equal, either. Credit unions generally offer better rates and benefits than do commercial banks, but not everyone is eligible to be a member of these credit unions. The two largest credit unions, United States Automobile Association (USAA) and Navy Federal Credit Union (NFCU), are excellent credit unions, and membership can often be acquired through either a family member, a friend, or a partner even if you didn't serve in the military. If you can get membership in either of these or perhaps in a credit union associated with your place of work, like a university or large company, then I would highly recommend that your two cards, or at least one of them, come from institutions like these. As a union the financial institution can offer you better rates, because members share, sometimes directly, in the overall financial well-being of the bank. This generally translates into better care being given to you and your money. Why it is so bad that you got into a situation requiring more advanced financial maneuvers and how we are going to get you out of a less than exemplary financial status is what I want to explore next.

Let us explore what is a lot of people's financial situation by looking at an example. Assuming you have decent credit, you may possess a credit card that has a published interest rate of around 10%. A quick note about interest rates is germane at this point, and will help you understand some terms that are often used in conjunction with credit cards. When a card publishes an interest rate you can't just use that number to figure out what you are actually paying them back in the form of interest, because of this nasty notion of compounding. Depending on how they compound, or apply, that interest they charge you, there is the notion of an *effective* annual percentage rate. In other words, what you are actually going to pay them as opposed to the published annual percentage rate of the card. If a card has a published rate of 14% as the annual percentage rate on a card somewhere in the very fine print, they will either mention an effective annual percentage rate or they will mention how often interest is applied. The reason it is important to understand compounding and effective annual interest rate and how it can hurt you is that you think you are paying one thing yet you are really paying a bit more. Most credit companies are in the business to make money so they compound interest on either a continuous basis (that is, the they only change the formula used to calculate to that little known e variable you may or may not have learned about) or on a daily basis. For example, with a card that publishes a 14% annual percentage interest rate, you are really effectively getting, if they compound daily, an effective interest rate of about 15.02%. In other words, more than 14% will actually be subtracted from your payments. Put another way, you will pay them back slightly more, 1.02%, than the 14% you thought they were tacking on to your overall payments in one year. That 1.02% may not seem like a lot, but as the balance gets higher, it is more of your money being taken out of each monthly payment for servicing your debt. Also, even during those days when you are not paying anything, the interest is compounding, which you will see in a minute. Anyway, back to our notional credit card. Let's assume you have a modest balance on that card, say $5000. They are only going to charge you about 2% each month as a minimum monthly payment that *theoretically* will pay off your balance after some period of time. One hundred dollars a month doesn't sound like a lot, especially considering that you were able to purchase a new big-screen TV or some other such luxury. The problem is the hidden cost for that debt, that is, the interest they compound or add to the standing balance. Interest on a credit card compounds generally daily, as I mentioned. It is this compounding that makes the debt so devastating and why it keeps you poorer than you would like to be. Looking at our example again, if you pay just 100 dollars a month, it's going to take you almost 5 ½ years to pay off that debt and you will pay almost $1500 in interest for that debt plus, of course, the $5000 they lent you in the first place. Put another way, what do you lose each month, and why does it take so long to pay off that debt? The reason is that while you aren't paying anything the debt is still accruing interest, which makes your periodic payment worth a little less. I like to see things in a series so that I really see what is happening to my money. So, let us look at this debt over just one month:

| | | | |
|---|---|---|---|
| 1 | $5,000.00 | 16 | $5,020.59 |
| 2 | $5,001.37 | 17 | $5,021.96 |
| 3 | $5,002.74 | 18 | $5,023.34 |
| 4 | $5,004.11 | 19 | $5,024.72 |
| 5 | $5,005.48 | 20 | $5,026.09 |
| 6 | $5,006.85 | 21 | $5,027.47 |
| 7 | $5,008.22 | 22 | $5,028.85 |
| 8 | $5,009.60 | 23 | $5,030.22 |
| 9 | $5,010.97 | 24 | $5,031.60 |
| 10 | $5,012.34 | 25 | $5,032.98 |
| 11 | $5,013.72 | 26 | $5,034.36 |
| 12 | $5,015.09 | 27 | $5,035.74 |
| 13 | $5,016.46 | 28 | $5,037.12 |
| 14 | $5,017.84 | 29 | $5,038.50 |
| 15 | $5,019.21 | 30 | $5,039.88 |
| | | 31 | $4,941.26 |

As you can see here, that $5000 you started with at the beginning of the month got to be $5039.88 before you even made your first payment. Then you pay $100 dollars because you want to pay your bill on time; otherwise, they will hike up your interest rate and charge you a late fee—all things we definitely want to avoid during the time we carry this balance. But that $100 payment got the overall debt only down to $4941.26 at the end of the month.

In other words, the bank took just about $40 of your payment for themselves and then applied the rest to your debt's balance, which is called principal. Then the whole process starts the very next day, now with a starting balance of $4941.26. I am not saying they are doing anything to directly hurt you, but doesn't that reduce your monthly income? You gave 100 dollars of your income, but the bank took $40 right off the top. Wouldn't you like to have that $40? I know I would. This example is for someone with decent credit. It should be noted that, technically, this example displays the second month of your debt, because credit cards often offer you a grace period of about 30 days to pay off the debt. But if you could afford the $5000 TV simply 30 days later, then I think you would have probably waited and just bought it 30 days later. The example I have outlined here is only designed to depict what a debt on a credit card looks like and how they make money and why it takes you much longer to pay off the debt than you would think. Also, if you are getting that TV at an even higher rate, the bank is taking more of your payment *before* applying the rest to the loan's principal. In fact, if any of the variables change upward, the situation for you gets only worse. A higher interest rate or longer terms help the bank, not you. No one tells you this when they tell you debt is bad. I didn't listen to those people and I bought the TV, and many other things. This landed me in a situation with a whole lot more debt and with the bank taking a whole lot more of my payments from my modest income.

This brings me to another important point about payments to credit cards, and that is *when* you should make your payment. Usually credit cards become due around the middle of the month. In my example above your payment would be due around day 15 not day 31, but it still would accrue about 30 days' worth of interest from the previous 30 days. What is important to take into consideration is that if you have the money sooner than the due date, as long as it is still within your budget, you should make the payment as soon as you can. Typically, people get paid twice a month, or on a biweekly periodicity. What this could mean is that you may get a paycheck on, say, the 10th of the month, but because your payment is not due until the 15th, you may wait to pay it. Financial institutions have made making your payments easier with the advent of things like scheduled online bill payments. With these programs you can make your payment on just about any day you want, but should you wait until the 15th or should you arrange for the payment to arrive on the 11th? The answer to this question is to pay it on the 11th. In fact, you should pay it as soon as you can each month, because, as described above, the institution is taking interest based on the principal and the sooner you make the payment, the sooner you shave off some of the principal upon which the next day's interest is calculated. All of this is key to principal reduction and, in turn, paying less interest for the borrowed money. In the example above, you can see that each day they charge you about $1.37 (slightly more as you now know because it is calculated on the previous day's balance), so if you pay your bill on the 11th instead of the 15th, you would get charged 10% on a lower balance on day 12. This would amount to something slightly less than $1.37 on day 12 and then it would start to creep up again until you make next month's payment. It is similar to the circumstance in which the owner of the loan for your house offers for you pay to your mortgage twice a month versus once a month. This will take years off your mortgage because the principle applies to your home mortgage as well. You can take time off the overall amortization, because interest is calculated off the previous day's balance here, too. The problem is that a mortgage is a big purchase, so paying twice a month may make a bigger dent in your monthly budget, which you may not be able to support. But if you can pay your mortgage twice a month with smaller payments each time, then you should try to set it up that way.

The point to understand at this juncture is this: don't wait to make your payments for anything that accrues interest. If you have gotten paid then make a payment soon thereafter so that you can erode as much of the principal as you can before they start charging you interest again. There are two matters to be aware of, though. If you are making a payment early in a given payment cycle, the bank may not assume that the payment was for the next month's bill, so make sure when you make any payments that they are reflected correctly on your statements. For example, it should say in your statements that you owe zero as your minimum payment if you already paid it, even if you paid it early. If it still says you owe something, then they may have applied that payment differently. It will still be going toward paying down your debt, but the bank may not recognize it as the next month's payment. As I mentioned before, you don't want any payments to be late, and not monitoring if a payment has been made is an easy way to overlook such a thing. You may get charged a late fee and you will retard the good work you have been doing by paying down your debt. This is especially important in relation to your mortgage. If you don't specify where your payment should be applied, should you either pay early or pay over the minimum amount, it may not be applied to principal. It may be added to your escrow account and then you won't have done anything to erode your principal. Where your payment has been applied will be reflected in the monthly statement, but you want to ensure that it is going to the right place before that statement arrives, because it's much harder to direct it elsewhere once it has been applied. Also, mortgages often have a set amortization schedule and if you pay extra in a given month, that won't necessarily preclude you from having to pay the full amount of the next month's payment. That extra money may be reflected in an earlier payoff at the very tail end. On the other hand, it may be that you won't owe any money the next month if, for example, you make a payment that is twice the size of a normal monthly payment. The point is to watch mortgages a little more closely. If you pay more than the minimum required payment on an auto loan, the next month's statement will often say that you don't owe anything or your minimum payment will be less the following month. In this case, you should continue to pay at least what was your original monthly payment even if your billing statements says you don't owe anything. A bank's telling you that you don't owe anything is misleading. What the bank expects is a particular amount, as we discussed when I showed you a full amortization of a debt. If you pay something other than the minimum amount the following month, you will find yourself going back to the series of payments that give the bank the maximum amount of interest they can get off of your loan. Keep paying and not only will you knock down your overall loan, but the interest charged will be less overall.

The good news, though, is that banks, all of them, compete with each other. You can use this to your advantage to pay your debt off, not necessarily sooner, but hopefully for a little less interest. I don't care who holds my credit card debt, and I don't think you should either. What if you could pay off that $5000 without paying any interest, or a lot less interest? I am sure you are well aware of debt consolidation and debt relief and bankruptcy and their offers to do similar things, but I am not encouraging you to go down any of these routes. You don't need to, and you don't need to damage your credit for a long period of time.

Unfortunately, credit scores seem to be linked to nearly everything we do these days. If your credit is already bad, you are going to have a hard time employing my methods, but, trust me, there is still much you can do. I will give you some tips to help you clean up your credit fairly quickly, but first let's deal with paying that $5000 at a much lower interest rate, if we can.

If you have another card that doesn't carry a balance, that is going to be your key to this maneuver. If you followed my advice on how to establish credit and use credit cards, this option will be available to you. Make sure you are making your payments on time and continue to do so; not paying on time once could put you back at square one, having to reestablish credit, and we do not want that.

Generally, at some point during the year your bank with the card that doesn't have a balance on it is going to notice it doesn't have a balance, and banks have gotten into the habit of offering either introductory rates or balance-transfer rates that are much lower than their normal rates. You need to seize upon these rates and opportunities. The banks usually have a period of time for which they will offer you this lower interest rate, like a year. There are some terms you should be familiar with if you are going to do any balance transfers or any maneuvers I am suggesting and they are: convenience checks, balance transfers, cash advances, and any fees associated with the transfer. Let us look at each of them in turn.

Convenience checks are just a vehicle to effect the transfer of money or to pay someone for something that then becomes a debt on your credit card. Sometimes there is a fee associated with using these checks, and, strangely, the physical size of these checks is generally larger than traditional checks. These convenience checks are fairly versatile, because, like the little checks associated with your bank account, they can be written to anyone for just about anything. The fees are usually something like $75 dollars or 3% of the amount of the check, generally the lesser of the two. Make no mistake, though, once you write one of these checks and it is cashed, you will have a debt on your credit card. But if used correctly, this is one method of transferring a balance to a bank with more reasonable terms, which will help you in the long run. They can be used to get a debt without a traditional account number put on terms you can monitor, track, and, hopefully, save money on. We will discuss the benefits of this type of debt consolidation, but for now just be familiar with the terminology banks use for this financial vehicle.

Balance transfers are another method of moving the money off one bank's ledger and on to another bank's books. Much of what occurs when you do a balance transfer is transparent to you, but another financial institution will own the debt after the transfer occurs. This means that the new financial institution will have the rights, like collection, as well as any interest gains that the previous institution had. It also means that if you decide to stop paying this institution, they will go after you just like the other one did.

Instead of trying to avoid the debt, use this method to secure better terms so that you can pay it off sooner. These are not like convenience checks and can only be used for things that have accounts. You can't just pay your friend or buy something without having already set up an account with that institution. There are sometimes fees associated with these, and sometimes the bank treats these as cash advances. If they do carry it as a cash advance, it will have an interest rate that is *higher* than the normal rate for purchases, and that doesn't do you any good. Although, sometimes they will do that only after an introductory period or they may still call it a cash advance, but will assign a special introductory interest rate to it. That is why I say wait for any "offers", or ask to see if they have any available. It is these offers of low interest rate balance transfers that will provide the greatest resource for you to pay down your debts. Sometimes these offers are even part of your account dashboard when you access your account online and all you need to do is click a tab or a link and it will take you to a page of these offers as well as offers for things like car loans, home loans or refinances, or other credit card transactions. Some balance transfers are treated as cash advances and even when they are not they can come with fees. This is the time to read carefully exactly what they are offering. Some offers they make available to you waive the cash advance fees and extend either reduced interest rates or rates even as low as zero for a period of time. That is the type of cash advance you are after.

    I outlined most of the fees associated with the vehicles banks offer you to borrow, transfer, or substitute one loan for another, but there are certainly more. Banks are getting more and more creative. Again, just be sure to read carefully what fees are associated with any offer you are looking to accept. The fees must be considered when transferring balances from one card to the next and then potentially back again. If these fees are high enough, you shouldn't flop balances back and forth too often otherwise all of your hard work in getting a low rate will only be lost in transaction fees to shift the balance. Strive to get the longest term possible on any of these low or no interest periods so that you aren't paying a bunch of fees in the place of high interest. There is one potential pitfall that you just need to be aware of so that you don't fall into it. It has to do with the way banks accept payments. It happens in a scenario where you have a large amount of money from one of the methods I outline or some other resource and you choose to use that money to make big payment on your debt, but you don't necessarily pay it off. The way to avoid the pitfall is if you have money to make a big payment, make sure you make that *before* you accept the offer and transfer balances or pay off one card with another through any of the vehicles mentioned. You may want to do this is so that you can free up the whole balance on a card before you use it to consolidate your debt on this one card's offer. If you carry a balance, accept the offer, and then make a big payment, the bank will, more often than not, apply the big payment to the special offer balance instead of the balance carrying your normal rate of interest. This is the very opposite way you would intend for them to do that, but once they do it there is little chance of reversing it. They will tell you this is just how it is done; I will tell you it is to ensure that they make as much money as possible. They don't like the offer rate, because they make less money off it than they would if that balance was at the regular rate, but they still make some money. The balance of that debt is on their ledger and not their competitors, but how you pay it back to them is largely at their discretion. Make that large payment so it dents your normal interest rate balance first, and wait to make sure that payment posts first, then accept the offer and do the maneuver so that there is no chance of that bigger payment being applied to the new introductory rate instead of the regular rate. This will unravel the whole reason to do the balance transfer, because it will essentially leave you right back where you started. It seems intuitive, but lots of people overlook this and then they find themselves at the wrong end of the debt again.

Going back to our example, and assuming you have found one of these offers that has a lower or non-existent rate, you can now transfer that $5000 balance—or in fact a lesser amount since you have been making your payments—to the bank with the offer. Once you do this you now have some choices to make. One option is to try to pay more to the new card so that you can pay the whole balance off within the introductory period, or, strangely, the other option is to pay less. Making larger payments makes sense, because you will eradicate the debt more quickly, and you will give yourself a greater chance of paying off that balance during the introductory period. The option of paying less requires a little more explanation. If you pay less, or if you pay the minimum required payment on that debt, you can now pay more to service other debts you have, like another card or a store card carrying a higher interest rate, or whatever other debts you have. If you decide to pay less, because your minimum required payments will likely go down, I wouldn't suggest using that extra money to get yourself into greater debt, but so long as you can continue to get these offers you should be able to keep even that new debt less painful.

You also have to be mindful of the other card you transferred the balance from, because what if you are approaching the end of the offer period and you still have some balance left on the card you used to pay the first card? Perhaps because you chose to attack other debts and paid only the minimum amount to the card holding the transferred balance. If this happens there is good news for your either way. The first card will likely have a similar balance transfer offer at some point, and you can use this to transfer that remaining balance back to that card provided they offer a rate better than what the balance was originally carried or will carry once the introductory period is over. Ping-ponging the debt from one card to the next until you pay it off entirely interest free or at a very low interest rate should be your goal. All of this is a way you can still spend the $5000, but get to pay it back over time without incurring costly interest fees. As mentioned before, don't do this too often, but you may need to do it a couple of times before the debt is fully paid off. I am not loyal to any of my banks. I am only loyal to being able to pay off the pile of debt at, hopefully, a low interest rate, paying as much toward reducing the principal as possible. I don't care who holds the claim to my pile of debt. To me, in this respect, one bank is as evil or as good as the next. So now what do you do if you don't have a second credit card to help pay off the first debt or debts?

Sometimes you will be offered these lower rates as part of a balance transfer in conjunction with an application for a new credit card. Financial counselors will caution you to not use this method, but I disagree, provided you do it right. If you have only one credit card, I see no reason why you shouldn't take advantage of an opportunity to pay your debts at a lower rate for 6 months or longer, even if the rate goes back up after that period of time, as I will explain later. You should certainly consider the rate after the introductory period though. If it is close to what you were paying on your first card then again who cares who owns the debt, because you managed to pay down some of the debt with a lower introductory rate until the rate goes up. If that rate is a great deal more than what you were paying previously, then either keep looking for a card with a better rate after the introductory period ends or look around for another card to transfer whatever balance you have left after the introductory period. The first card you transferred the balance from may have an offer that you can take advantage of or you can look to get one more credit card with a good introductory period offer. Don't go past a third card though, because the more credit cards you carry past two can start to negatively affect your credit rating and we need a decent credit rating to help us pay down our debts.

Another thing to take into consideration is whether that introductory period carries deferred interest. This is one time you will need to ensure you can pay off the card or transfer the balance before that introductory period ends. Deferred interest is not the same as zero or low interest, because if the interest is only being deferred, then if you don't pay it off during the introductory period, you will not only be at a higher rate but they will resurrect and add to your balance all of the interest benefits you got during the introductory period. That is not what you want, because that negates all the benefits you got from paying less or having more of your money going to the principal of the debt instead of to the interest. Now you will be stuck with the debt, the deferred interest amount you didn't have to pay until now, and typically a higher interest rate. There are only two circumstances where I would recommend that you accept an offer of lower or no interest for a deferred introductory period: if you know for sure that you can pay off the balance during the deferment period or, failing that, if you know that you can transfer the balance from the deferred-interest card to another card before the deferment period ends. If you have gotten to this point and still have not found a method that works for you to pay down your debt, don't despair, because there are still ways to pay off your debt for less than it would cost to pay it directly, and that is the topic of our next chapter.

# CHAPTER 3—PAYING OFF DEBTS OTHER WAYS

*Unlike today where you can determine your financial situation the minute you make a transaction or a point of sale when I was a child the fact that we were poor was only tangentially obvious to me. There were times when it became much clearer, and grocery shopping was one of them. We would walk to the store to get groceries and then walk back carrying whatever provisions we had acquired. They were not in the much easier to carry plastic bags of today either. The only bags available were paper bags, which didn't even have handles like they do now, and even if they did have handles wet vegetables would quickly erode the handle spilling the contents everywhere anyway. They also employed baggers to bag your groceries, and being in a small town the people bagging these goods were generally people I knew from my high school, and not just the rank and file folks like myself, but people like the Associate Student Body (ASB) president or the Capitan of the football team. During these socially turbulent years the last thing you want to do is draw upon yourself negative attention, however, either my mother was unaware of such pressures or she simply ignored them. She had no reservations about yelling my name in the grocery store when she either: needed something from another isle or just needed to know my general location. Again, unlike today when I can't find my son and quietly text him to tell me where he is, she had a particularly cutting voice and it would penetrate at least 7 isles of groceries and knife its way into ears of first, the ASB president then, his or her network of social contacts, and nearly find its way to morning school announcements. I didn't help matters since I tried to ignore these calls and tried to make it seem like it was clearly someone else she was calling for who only coincidentally shared my name. I would rapidly turn my head from side to side looking for another recipient of these sonic booms. Even to this day I don't like to hear my name, and I place the blame for such self-deprecation squarely on my mother's shoulders. When the collecting the goods was completed the persecution did not end. My mother would make a point of ensuring the heavier items were, "double bagged because we are walking". This only served to display a balance to our checking account that hovered closer to zero than everyone else around us in line, or at least so I thought. Interestingly, today, I, too, have even uttered the same words regarding the bagging of my goods. Double bagging does not have the stigma it once had. Today, with a greater focus on the environmental impacts of both people and consumables double bagging, because you are walking, has become something of a yuppie or, at least, socially conscious upper middle class thing to do. Don't we all want to be in that category?*

While using another credit card to pay off debt is probably the cleanest way to execute one debt with another, it does have some disadvantages. Credit agencies still register the new debt until it is completely paid off. The things we will discuss in this chapter help pay off the debt, and, simultaneously, help to improve your credit score. The first utilizes the greatest, and most useful, purchase you will likely make in your life, and that is a mortgage.

A mortgage is not only useful in providing you a place to live, but it is one of the very few purchases you will make that resembles more of an investment than just a purchase. Most people must leverage themselves, in other words, go into debt, to purchase a house, and you will certainly pay some interest over the course of this loan and some fees. Unlike other things you purchase though, you can take some of that interest and the property taxes you pay off your income taxes. That asset is also likely to increase in value over time. This equity can be used to purchase another house when you sell your current house, it can be used to pay down other debts, it can be used to fund other things like businesses or other endeavors you might want to do, and many other things. Your first thought may be to think that if one house is good then seven houses are better, and this may incentivize you to become a house flipper or hope to make your fortunes off owning rental properties. While these schemes make work for some, I am not going to advise you to go down either of those paths simply because they come with their own set of challenges. Flipping houses is fine—if you flip them, but there is some work that goes into preparing the house for sale again, and you are more susceptible to the ebb and flow of the markets. It can easily become more onerous than the job you currently have, and could end up costing you your financial position if you do it wrong. Again, I am only trying to help you live the life *you* want, not suggesting you change your career to something you may not want.

Rental properties come with even more challenges—namely, renters. Renters are a special breed of people in that they do not have the same motivations you do with your house, or really with anything you own and maintain. It is their place of residence, but it is not their house. Much like the old saying that the fastest car is a rental car, because no one really cares how that car performs after they turn it back into the rental company. Rental cars can be driven to the very limits of their performance while they have it for a week, and then it becomes someone else's problem. Your rental properties are very similar, however, unlike a car which has standard options a rental home comes with certain living standards that you, not the renter, must provide. If the roof leaks on your own home you will fix it, but there is a good chance that your two other rental homes also may need roof repairs at the exact same time. If you want renters to stay, and help pay for your mortgage on those homes, you will have to fix the roofs of these other homes as well. The costs can quickly outweigh the benefits. I personally don't want the headache, but be my guest if you do. You will get similar benefits from these rental investments to the ones I am about to outline, but the bank knows this as well, and they want to ensure they collect the debts you incur buying these extra homes. They will charge you more interest for these extra homes. There is a special investment interest rate that is not as low as the one you get on your primary residence or even your vacation home. If you are going to buy an extra house, I wouldn't go past a vacation home.

    The house you buy as your primary residence, though, can help you with your other debts or help you live a lifestyle slightly above your means, but just like with brownies, don't abuse it. The gluttonous days of lore are somewhat behind us, so, unlike in early 2000 to 2009, expect that you will need to have a job, some savings, not a lot of debt, and a credit score in the 640 or above range to qualify for a mortgage loan. If you don't have those things or are already in a deep debt hole you can probably push to another section of this chapter to find other means to pay down that debt, and get you back in a positon to be able to qualify for a mortgage in the future. The first house you buy won't be your dream home either, or perhaps it will, but if you frame it in the context of the fact that you are starting on a path to your dream home then perhaps it will be a little more palatable. Banks apply a greater level of scrutiny to your financial history than they did just before the housing bust, and while seemingly painful at the time of your application, the pain will end, and hopefully you will be in your purchased home soon enough. Applying and getting the house, while not exactly a straight line, is fairly standard so I won't lecture you about home inspections, escrow, down payments and closing costs other than to say that you should familiarize yourself with the terms of a home purchase just like you would familiarize yourself with the terms of the trade if you were buying a car or buying a computer. What I will draw your attention to is some of the costs associated with a home so that you understand, financially, how they will affect you.

You know you will be paying interest to purchase the house, and while I agree how much you pay is important, it is not the only thing to consider. While there are plenty of people you will encounter just before or after your home purchase who will almost immediately ask you, "what rate did you get," I don't think it should be your primary concern. Whatever interest rate you get must be considered in conjunction with the income tax rate bracket you fall into as well as how long you are going to keep then home. As I said before, you will get back some of this interest, which has the effect of lowering this listed interest rate. Let us look at a concept that will affect you right away though. If, for example, you are paying an interest rate of 4% on a loan of $200,000 you will pay about $950 dollars a month for the mortgage and interest, but if you don't put anything toward the house by way of a down-payment you will likely pay Private Mortgage Insurance (PMI). This will be on top of that $950, and it could be something like $120 more a month just for that insurance. Private Mortgage Insurance is just another hedging opportunity, for the bank, to ensure they make their money. If you have less than 20% equity in your home, in other words, you don't own outright 20% of the value of the home, you are a riskier investment for the bank than is someone who does own 20% of the home they purchase. It has to do, basically, with the fact that you are less likely to walk away from something that you own 20% of than if you do not. There is certainly some truth to this notion, but the problem with PMI is it is a total loss for you. It does not do you any good and, unlike the mortgage interest, you can't deduct any of it, and it doesn't help your credit either. You want to try very hard to avoid paying it. Veterans Administration (VA) home backed loans, generally, don't require PMI. Some credit unions offering mortgages do not either, but, generally, the less you put into the home, in the form of a down-payment, the more risk the bank has, and the greater the chance they will require PMI. It, too, should not deter your dream to own a home though, and I will show you why. This is about what the mortgage example outlined above will look like over the first year:

| | | |
|---|---|---|
| 1 | $200,000.00 | |
| 2 | $199,711.67 | $666.67 |
| 3 | $199,422.37 | $665.71 |
| 4 | $199,132.11 | $664.74 |
| 5 | $198,840.89 | $663.77 |
| 6 | $198,548.69 | $662.80 |
| 7 | $198,255.52 | $661.83 |
| 8 | $197,961.37 | $660.85 |
| 9 | $197,666.24 | $659.87 |
| 10 | $197,370.13 | $658.89 |
| 11 | $197,073.03 | $657.90 |
| 12 | $196,774.94 | $656.91 |
| | | $7,279.94 |

That seems like a lot of interest that you paid over the year, and frankly it is, but you do get a portion of that $7279.94 back in the form of a slightly lower tax bill. Without overcomplicating it by showing you how it would affect you individually let us just say it is a decent amount, and depending on your tax bracket it could be more. The reason it can lower your tax bill is you get to deduct this amount off of your Adjusted Gross Income (AGI) and then they apply the tax obligation for which you are responsible. This is similar to how you are charged for things, like health insurance, in your paychecks, if it is employee sponsored.

It is important to note that you can only take this deduction if you itemize when you fill out your tax return. Itemizing is when you separate qualifying expenses separately in calculating your taxable income as opposed to taking the standard deduction. If you do not have expenses that will put you over the standard deduction levels, which vary for singles, head of household, and married couples who file jointly, you won't get the tax break. In other words, you don't get to itemize your deductions. This becomes an important consideration for many people in the middle income range, because if you don't exceed the standard deduction then it may be better to, instead, rent, and use the extra money that you are not paying in a mortgage and invest that money so that your station in life can be elevated to such a point that you can afford a home mortgage with interest charges that exceed the standard deduction. In all likelihood, it won't be terribly difficult to exceed the standard deduction should you buy a home, but it is certainly something to investigate before you do. There is also the equity benefits of buying a home, so despite not getting the tax break I still think, since you need to have some place to live, it makes sense to buy a home at some point. The deduction for the interest you paid is not a credit either, so you do not get to take the amount out of your tax bill like you would for a tax credit. It is, therefore, not a one-to-one relationship. The reason is because of the way your taxes are calculated. It depends, again, on your tax bracket, and then you must compare that amount to what you would have gotten had you taken the standard deduction to see if you are really getting a better deal. Say, for example, you paid $13,000 dollars in mortgage interest and were married, but in the 25% tax bracket. In other words, your two incomes, combined, total less than (in 2017) $91,900. You would be getting only about ¼ of that interest in the form of a tax break back, so about $3250. If you had taken the standard deduction (in 2017) you could have used the standard deduction of $12,700 and gotten about ¼ of that off your tax bill which is about $3175. As you can see you are only getting a net-benefit of about $75 dollars over the standard deduction for the $13,000 you spent in interest. To me, that still beats giving it to someone else in the form of rent since you will be paying rent if you decide not to buy a home. Also, in order to do a full accounting of the benefits you receive, one must also take into consideration the equity you got from owing the home. Over time this adds up even if you only get a tax break of $75 dollars a year. If the house goes up in value by $5000 in that first year, and you paid back some principal over the same year, let us see how much you benefit. In our example, that amounted to $3226 ($200,000-$196,774). Your benefit is ($5000 + $3226 + $75) or $8301. The $75 is a realized gain and while the $8226 is unrealized, or not directly available to you until you sell the home, it is still value you can use on your behalf or when you sell the home. This is why I still think it is advantageous to buy a home at some point in your life, if you can. The new tax law changes recently passed under the Trump administration will change some of this so, obviously, do the same kind of comparison once those laws start to take effect and more is known about what it will do to housing deductions and corresponding tax implications. Now, back to our loan example.

This is a loan amortized (calculated with both principal and interest) over 30 years or 360 months. Once you make that final payment on the first of the 360$^{th}$ month you will own your home outright, but these days I do not think people buy one home and stay in it 360 months or until they die anymore, and then have it pass down to their children. Jobs, well more directly, the economy, forces us to move to where money can be made. Other things like relationships, jobs shifting locations, high divorce rates, and children could also motivate us to change our location over our lifetime, but that is quite acceptable. You are paying down the principal of your loan while they are charging you interest. See for yourself, at the end of the first year, you own about 1.6% of your home—be proud. Next year you will own more and the following, even more. As you can also see, the part you are giving to the bank is decreasing as well. Most of your interest is paid in the early years, and this is by design, so that the bank can start making more money to loan other people money so that they can make even more money. It is this small amount of equity that is of real value to you, because while I say you own 1.6% of you home in that first year, you may in fact own a little more. Homes tend to rise in value over time. There are periods when they will go down, and as a victim of the housing bust in 2008-2009, I can tell you they can go down a lot. Like any investment, though, time is your friend. If they go down during a period that can be offset by them going up in later periods. If, and I am not saying, if like when one says, "if you jump off a building you might not die," but rather, with a positive connotation. If the value of your home goes up, you get this value—not the bank. It is something, I am sure, they look at with great chagrin.

Unfortunately the bank is the only one looking to get a little piece of your future. The city gets some in the form of property taxes. These are often overlooked costs of a home, because they are buried in your mortgage payment. You don't just pay about $950 dollars a month for that home you bought. You pay more, because the mortgage company collects escrow on your behalf to pay the city its property taxes, again, on your behalf. The city doesn't care who they get the money from, but I suspect they prefer it comes from the mortgage company since they only have to cash one check for some thousands of homes in the city upon which a particular bank holds the mortgage. I cannot tell you what those costs are exactly, but on a $200,000 home you will probably pay something, like, $2500 dollars a year, paid in quarterly installments through your mortgage bank. The city is eagerly watching your home's value as well so let us talk about them briefly.

Each year the city tax assessor will do an assessment of home values in your area, not unlike a realtor would, but the difference is the city doesn't really care if you can sell your home for the value they assign it or not; they only care if they can charge you more property tax on that increase in value. If the city the following year thinks the value of your home is $210,000, you will be charged more for property tax than you were charged in the year the home was worth $200,000. This extra charge will be passed along to you through your mortgage company, because they sure as heck are not going to pay this extra amount for you. Your monthly mortgage payment will go up, because the bank has its own set of internal rules on escrow accounts, and how much must be in them. They will not be caught without enough money in that escrow account to pay your property taxes. My advice with tax assessments is to definitely look at this piece of correspondence you get once a year, because there is recourse if they value your house higher than its market value or, at least, higher than it really is valued by any definition. On this letter there is likely to be a way to file an appeal, and the person doing the assessment is just a person like you, with a job much like yours. You can set up an appointment to see how they valued your home. I suggest you come prepared for this appointment, because they may or may not be prepared. I did this one year and my assessor was not as well prepared as I was, which played to my favor. In his defense, he has hundreds, if not thousands, of homes to look at, while I only have to look at my one home. It was not hard to get prepared either, because in this day of the internet a pretty accurate market value of your home can be found very easily. Some places use a different formula, but is hard to argue against market value since it is really what people will pay for the home that determines value, at least with regard to property. He had a list of similar homes, and you can question these comparison homes, because if they are not comparable then they ought not be using it in their comparison. This could happen if not a lot of homes in your neighborhood have sold. A realtor is going to do a more thorough job of ensuring your home is properly valued, because their commission is tied to it. This is not the case for the city employee. If you do not like the value he or she has assigned to your property, then fight it, because once it is registered at a particular value it is a whole lot harder to go back and change it. In my case, they had valued my home, in my opinion, about $50,000 more than it really should have been. This was significant enough, in my opinion, for me to speak to the tax assessor. He was nice enough, but as I said, not prepared. I showed him comparable home and their values which were not $50,000 more, and about 2 weeks later I received an amended letter which showed a value that was exactly the number I had purported was the value of my home. Your goal, while you own the home, is to have the tax value be as low as possible while the market value is a high as possible. Certainly don't do anything illicit to get them to be mismatched, but that market value is the realized gains you would get if you sold the home, and if the tax bill on that value is less then you benefit with realized savings since you are not just giving it to the city. Again, don't let any of this deter you from owning a home, because, after all, you need some place to live. If you rent, you are just allowing someone else to do all of this for you while taking all the equity for themselves.

Closing costs are also something to consider when buying your home. They are costs that you also lose, and they can be significant if you refinance your house many times to tap that equity in order to pay other things or if you indeed want to sell the home, and are now looking to realize your gains. Closing costs on a $200,000 home can still be around $6000, and you don't get to reclaim any of this either. Definitely bear this in mind if you decide to use refinancing as a method for paying down your debt, because each time you refinance and tap some of your equity both the amount you can tap goes down and you lose the closing costs to perform the transaction.

Another entity that gets money from you owning a home is your home insurance company. This costs also becomes part of your escrow payments and is usually paid once a year. It varies, like all insurance, on the value of the house as well as where the house is located. If you are in an area prone to home damage, like, say, a fault line or Tornado Ally, or even a flood plain, the insurance company takes this into consideration and passes the cost to cover such damage on to those they insure. Just like if you lease a car, as opposed to buying the car outright, you are required to carry extra coverage for not being able to pay for your home outright. Since you don't really own your home the bank wants to make sure if the home is damaged you don't just walk away from your debt, and the home. That is why if you finance a home the bank will require you to have homeowner's insurance. You probably want to have homeowner's insurance anyway, because it can help you with various things that may befall you while you own the property; even if you buy the home outright and are not required to carry homeowner's insurance. It is one of the few insurances you will actually use as opposed to just carrying. If you are also having a cash flow problem, like your car insurance, you can increase the deductible on your homeowner's insurance policy which may lower your insurance and, in turn, lower your mortgage payments. Since this will shield the insurance company from having to pay for small claims you might make they will pass that savings on to you. The only thing to be aware of is if you really do need to use it you will have to have, as cash, whatever deductible you designate available to pay for part of the claim. Don't make it so high you can't make any claims on your home insurance. Trust me, you will probably use this more than you will use your car insurance.

The things we just talked about comprise what I term *PIPE*. It is just an easy mnemonic to remember all of the things that comprise what you actually pay in your mortgage payment:

P-for *P*rinciple, I-for *I*nterest, P-for *P*MI (if applicable), and E-for *E*scrow

The reason I use this mnemonic is because mortgage companies and many mortgage calculators don't clearly articulate what all is included in your mortgage payment. I suspect you want to know exactly what, and to whom, you are paying your payment each month, because it is your money that funds all of the elements of *PIPE*. Escrow, for payment of property taxes and homeowner's insurance, is usually the thing most often left off either a calculator or someone calculating your mortgage payments for you. If the calculator, or person you are using to calculate your mortgage payment, either asks for your zip code or directly asks to estimate your property taxes it, or he/she, is probably going to give you a better estimate of your actual mortgage payment. Often, the house listing will list what the property taxes were the previous year so you can use that to estimate. Just don't let someone selling you a mortgage tell you what your complete mortgage payment is unless you have verified, at least, all the elements of *PIPE* are accounted for.

    Points are something else lenders will offer you when you buy a home so you should have some familiarity with how they work, and how they can affect you. Points work differently depending, again, on your perspective. From your perspective it is a way to lower the interest rate the lender charges you to buy the home. For example, they will list a loan's Annual Percentage Rate (APR) as 4.5% with no points and 4.25% if you pay 1 point. The "point" costs you money at closing. It is giving the lender money now so they lower your interest rate on the loan over the life of the loan, and you save money. At least that is the idea. Why would the lender offer to lower your interest rate? The reason, from their perspective is because they can take that money you give them at closing and invest it elsewhere, and make money on the money you are giving them now. In exchange, they allow you to pay less in interest for your home. It will lower your mortgage payment each month by an amount that is correlated to the points you pay. The problem I have with points is if I had an extra $2000 dollars that these points could cost at the time I wanted to buy a home, why wouldn't I just put that extra money down on the house to lower the amount I am borrowing or use that money to cover the host of applicable charges that go into the closing cost on a home. To actually recoup the cost you pay for the points you have to own the home for a period of time, again related to how many points you buy. There is what is known as a break-even point, or the amount of time you must own the home to recoup the cost of the points. If, say, you save 25 dollars a month in money you don't pay in interest because the bank offered you a lower interest rate because you bought one point for $2000 you have to wait $\frac{\$2000}{25\ per\ month} = 80\ months$ to recoup the $2000 you spent 80 months prior. That 80 months is 6 years and 9 months. That is a long time. As I said before, who knows how long you intend to be in your home, but in order to make it worth your $2000 you have to be in that home almost 7 years. Also, there is an opportunity cost to using that money to pay for points for a lower mortgage as opposed to taking that money and investing it yourself and making interest of your own over those same 7 years. I firmly believe your money could be put to better use than getting a monthly savings on the interest you pay on your mortgage. Also, since the government offers you a little bit of a tax break come income tax time, paying points makes that break smaller too, because you are paying less tax deductible interest. Remember, you get to adjust your yearly income a little by how much interest you paid on the mortgage. As you saw before, it isn't huge, but it could bring you to a negative split and you will not get the tax benefits if you buy too many points. If you pay less in interest then you get to take less out of your adjusted gross income. If you have all of this money lying around to pay points then you probably do not have the debts I address in this book and then probably do not need this book anyway. I wish that was the case, but most of us do not have a lot money to pay a lot, up front, on a house. You do not need the offer of points, you need the mortgage so that you can utilize it to pay off the other debts you have, and build your wealth, and oh, by the way, so that you can have a place to live in somewhere on this planet. Points are nice, but they, generally, cost more than they are worth. Now that we have covered most of the primary elements of a mortgage let us get back to why you want to buy a house, and what home ownership can do for you in the long run with respect to your other debts.

If the home we have been discussing, bought for $200,000, goes up in value then, as I mentioned before, you get that value, less what the city gets, but it is value nonetheless. If that home did go up to something reasonable, like $205,000, by the end of the first year then you really own a little over 4%. That is a 4% return on your investment—not bad for one year. It is this equity that is of value to you, at least, with regard to your debts. If you could not use the credit card swap method, and have racked up some debts after you purchased a home then there are circumstances which make refinancing, not selling and moving out of your home, sensible. Like, for example, if you are paying 180 dollars a month in interest on two credit cards over the course of a year you could be losing $4320 a year. Over two years that cost is going to now start to outweigh the cost of those closing costs we talked about if you refinancing your home. Refinancing can keep your mortgage payments near what you owe now, and you can utilize that equity to pay high interest debt. You just would, again, own less of your home, but you still get to stay there, of course. So what if you do not own a home or some other appreciating asset, how can you still crush your debts? One method is to use your work sponsored retirement account and the money contained in it.

In the retirement chapter we will go over how to better invest your hard earned money so that it works for you in retirement, but, for now, we need to get to our golden years with as little debt as possible, and one of the things at your disposal for this purpose is your Individual Retirement Account (IRA) in particular a 401(k). The difference being the 401(k) is employer sponsored and has its own set of rules and limits to contributions, and the use of those contributions. It can be used differently than an IRA and is, therefore, a valuable resource. While you can "roll over" your IRA for 60 days or even use it to buy the shares of a burgeoning company you start as another kind of roll over you generally cannot borrow against an IRA like you can your employer sponsored 401(k). Not all 401(k) plans allow you to borrow against them either, but if you can it is a very powerful tool. I understand most financial advisors will tell you not to touch these, and to leave them in for the long haul, but I disagree with leaving money in this savings account while you are literally bleeding out money in interest payments in another area.

## Financial Ninja

First, understand that I am not advocating using your retirement to pay down debt that is not significant, there are other ways of doing that, because your financial advisor is correct in that if you start early and leave your money in these kinds of accounts you will be rewarded handsomely in the future. Also, many employers that have these 401(k) programs will reduce their matching if you reduce your contribution below 5%. That is free money, so I would not reduce your contributions below 5% or whatever level your employer matches. In fact, I am not suggesting you reduce your contributions at all. I am, however, suggesting you can tap the money in this account to pay debts and then get back to saving for retirement. Loans from your retirement account are not like traditional loans and that is the reason why I am advocating their use. First let me outline the details of the types of retirement account loans available to you before I describe how to use them.

First there are rules on how much you can borrow and you have to meet specific requirements like:

- You need to have at least $1000 which is made up of contributions you make, not what your job matches, including the earnings on the money your job contributed.
- You have to continue to have your job for the duration of the loan. If you don't keep your job, quit, are let go, or fired, that loan will get turned into a distribution which is charged a 10% penalty and you will get charged income tax on that money as well. You will have 90 days to pay back the full loan before it gets charged against you. More on this later.
- You cannot have had a loan of the same type in the last 60 days. This is more recent rule, but I will explain how this could affect you.
- You can only borrow up to 50% of your total investment, but no more than $50,000. Much of this is based on IRS rules, one of which is the IRS $50,000 test. We will get into more detail on this later as well.

- You to have not borrowed more than $50,000 in the past 12 months. What this means is even if you have paid off a loan for $20,000 in the past year, you don't have another $50,000 available to you, but rather $30,000 until a full 12 months have passed since the $20,000 was borrowed. This one is important, because in order to use this money you have to be wise about how you do it so we will spend some time on this aspect.
- There is no penalty for paying the loan back early.
- Your spouse has rights to the money you borrow from this account, so don't think you can easily sneak money out of this account without your spouse knowing.

Most agencies let you borrow up to $50,000 and give you anywhere from 1 to 5 years to pay it back. Some agencies allow you to borrow this money to buy a primary residence, and they give you a period of 1 to 15 years to pay back these residential loans. You can also only have one loan of each type out at any time, but you can have one of each, meaning you can have a residential loan out and still borrow money to pay off some higher interest debts. The maximum amount for the both loans cannot total more than $50,000 though. The loan you take out will be charged interest, but the important thing is that this interest, unlike a traditional loan is deposited back into *your* account. In other words, it is not money lost to the bank as is the case with a traditional loan. I call this type of interest forced savings, because you are really paying yourself a penalty for borrowing the money, but I would much rather pay myself a penalty in the form of interest than I would a bank. Generally, these loans are made through your payroll department, and requesting the loan is usually quite simple. You just fill out the information on the website of your employer's 401(k) and once you fill in the online forms a check will be mailed to you. For some reason, currently, if you request direct deposit for these funds you will have to physically mail the request in so it really does not make sense to do so since you will be paying for that stamp, and it will take just as long to process. It will just be done on the front-end vice the back-end. If, of course, you don't have access to a computer you will have to do all of it through the mail, and that can delay the whole process as you will have to mail the request to them, they will have to process it, and then they will finally mail you a check back, and you can then finally deposit it and use it. The loan repayment is made in regular payments deducted from your pay each time you get paid. You are responsible for making sure the loan is being repaid though, so do not let your payroll department let it slide. If it gets taken out once though, you should be fine for the rest of the payments so you need to only ensure that they start the repayment. Generally, payments follow your pay schedule, so if you get paid biweekly, for example, they will space out the payments over that same period. The loan amortization schedule is usual available to see before you agree to accept the loan terms, and it will have the total amount of interest you will be paying on the loan—just remember this money isn't going to someone else. It is going back to you. The one thing that does get lost in this transaction is the processing fee. The processing fee is anywhere from $50 to $75 dollars, and that you do not get back so it should be considered when you are deciding to use this type of loan to pay off debt. Since you are only able to borrow your own contributions it takes a few years before this account will be of any real use to you, but as long as you followed my advice when you got the job and started investing in this account right away, as we will learn later, you should, hopefully, have a meaningful amount in this account should you find yourself with some debts. Those are the details of the loan, so when is it a good idea to use this asset to pay off some other debts carrying interest?

    Let us see if it would have been a good idea to use this to pay off the $5000 dollar TV we bought in our previous example. To do so we will use the same terms of that debt, namely it came at 10% interest and would take you about five-and-a-half years to pay off if you were making minimum payments. What we need to determine is if the loss of the investment interest we could have been making in our retirement account outweighs the interest we are losing on the loan for the TV, if it does not then it is a good idea. If it does then, of course, it is not. In other words, we don't want to lose more potential interest from our 401(k) then we are paying out in interest to the credit card. These same tools I will give you for this loan can be used for any loan up to the maximum loan amount of $50,000. You simply plug in the terms you are getting for your specific situation and see if it is reasonable, just as I will do with the $5000 loan. Again, I like to see the cash flow which will help us determine the validity of the idea. We will make some assumptions for my example that you will not need to make for your situation, because you will know the specifics of your situation. Use those numbers, not mine. Here is about what it looks like to pay it outright:

Financial Ninja

| Year 1 | | | Year 2 | | | Year 3 | | |
|---|---|---|---|---|---|---|---|---|
| 1 | $5,000.00 | | 1 | $4,267.01 | $36.09 | 1 | $3,457.26 | $29.40 |
| 2 | $4,941.67 | $41.67 | 2 | $4,202.57 | $35.56 | 2 | $3,386.07 | $28.81 |
| 3 | $4,882.85 | $41.18 | 3 | $4,137.59 | $35.02 | 3 | $3,314.29 | $28.22 |
| 4 | $4,823.54 | $40.69 | 4 | $4,072.07 | $34.48 | 4 | $3,241.91 | $27.62 |
| 5 | $4,763.73 | $40.20 | 5 | $4,006.00 | $33.93 | 5 | $3,168.93 | $27.02 |
| 6 | $4,703.43 | $39.70 | 6 | $3,939.39 | $33.38 | 6 | $3,095.33 | $26.41 |
| 7 | $4,642.63 | $39.20 | 7 | $3,872.21 | $32.83 | 7 | $3,021.13 | $25.79 |
| 8 | $4,581.32 | $38.69 | 8 | $3,804.48 | $32.27 | 8 | $2,946.30 | $25.18 |
| 9 | $4,519.49 | $38.18 | 9 | $3,736.19 | $31.70 | 9 | $2,870.86 | $24.55 |
| 10 | $4,457.16 | $37.66 | 10 | $3,667.32 | $31.13 | 10 | $2,794.78 | $23.92 |
| 11 | $4,394.30 | $37.14 | 11 | $3,597.88 | $30.56 | 11 | $2,718.07 | $23.29 |
| 12 | $4,330.92 | $36.62 | 12 | $3,527.86 | $29.98 | 12 | $2,640.72 | $22.65 |
| | | $430.92 | | | $360.86 | | | $283.46 |

| Year 3 | | | Year 4 | | | Year 5 | | |
|---|---|---|---|---|---|---|---|---|
| 1 | $2,562.73 | $22.01 | 1 | $1,574.52 | $13.84 | 1 | $482.84 | $4.82 |
| 2 | $2,484.08 | $21.36 | 2 | $1,487.64 | $13.12 | 2 | $386.86 | $4.02 |
| 3 | $2,404.78 | $20.70 | 3 | $1,400.04 | $12.40 | 3 | $290.08 | $3.22 |
| 4 | $2,324.82 | $20.04 | 4 | $1,311.71 | $11.67 | 4 | $192.50 | $2.42 |
| 5 | $2,244.20 | $19.37 | 5 | $1,222.64 | $10.93 | 5 | $94.11 | $1.60 |
| 6 | $2,162.90 | $18.70 | 6 | $1,132.83 | $10.19 | 6 | -$5.11 | $0.78 |
| 7 | $2,080.92 | $18.02 | 7 | $1,042.27 | $9.44 | 7 | | |
| 8 | $1,998.26 | $17.34 | 8 | $950.95 | $8.69 | 8 | | |
| 9 | $1,914.92 | $16.65 | 9 | $858.88 | $7.92 | 9 | | |
| 10 | $1,830.87 | $15.96 | 10 | $766.03 | $7.16 | 10 | | |
| 11 | $1,746.13 | $15.26 | 11 | $672.42 | $6.38 | 11 | | |
| 12 | $1,660.68 | $14.55 | 12 | $578.02 | $5.60 | 12 | | |
| | | $197.96 | | | $103.50 | | | $12.05 |

This totals about $1,389.00 in interest paid over the course of the loan, shown here in yearly totals. Now let us look at what we would make on the $5000 if we left it in our retirement account over the same period of time.

The future value of that $5000 in 5 years is about $6914 at an interest rate of 6.5%, meaning it would make about $1914 in investment interest. This is not quite directly comparable to the $1389, though, because it is not precisely what is happening to your investment or debt. What we really need to compare is if we were to pay back the $5000 over the course of the 5 years, and compare that loss to the loss of interest to the loan directly. Does the forced savings outweigh the loss of investment interest? I say only 5 years though because, you will recall, we cannot exceed 5 years to pay back this loan. In other words, it will get amortized over 5 years not 5 ½ years. You will have to pay yourself back that $5000. If you get paid biweekly you will pay about $83 a month for 60 months, or 5 years, but you have to include in those payments the extra interest that you pay to borrow from your retirement and the interest it is going to make on its own. If the interest rate they charge you at the time of the loan is 1.5% (not unreasonable for these types of loans) you are really getting an investment interest rate of 8% on this $5000 (the 6.5% it was earning plus the 1.5% penalty they charge you) over the 5 years on what you will pay to build back up to the $5000 you borrowed. The total you will have in your account after you pay back the $5000 in 5 years is about $6123. That is an additional $1123. Don't forget they charge you a fee to take this loan, so you really only make $1073 (less the $50 for the fee). Ok, now we have some numbers to compare:

|  | Cost | Benefit |
|---|---|---|
| Pay the credit card directly | $1,389 | |
| Interest you didn't make in retirement | $1,914 | |
| Interest you make paying yourself back | | $1,073 |

So what is our real cost of using the retirement account to pay off the debt and then paying ourselves back. We lose ($1914 − $1073 = $841). This is the interest we would have made if we had just left it in the account, but no longer do we lose the $1389 dollars in interest to the credit card company. So don't we actually gain ($1389 − $841 = $548)? Put another way, you did not lose the $1389 to the bank, and the portion of your retirement that you tapped netted a gain of $548 over the same period you would have lost $1389 to the bank. Also, you really gain a little bit more, because during the 6 months you are still paying the credit card company, your little nest egg will have been repaid and will make approximately another $200, because it will still be growing. Ok, what about monthly? How are you faring there? Monthly you are doing slightly better as well, because instead of paying the bank $100 a month (the minimum payments) you are only paying about $84 a month, which is a cash flow increase of $16 each month that you can use to pay off other things. Your credit score will also improve as well, because you don't have the $5000 in debt according to the credit reporting agencies. The loan you took from your retirement is not part of their calculations. This will possibly enable you to now use the two credit card method to pay other debts more quickly that we talked about earlier. Your retirement account will still be growing also because these loans are in addition to your normal contributions. It is this that can help you pay off more debt. Just don't quit your job or get fired, because you will have 90 days to pay back that loan entirely otherwise it will be a distribution from the account and charged a penalty of 10% on top of the income tax you will pay on the amount you still have to pay back. This 10% penalty only applies if you are under 59 ½ though, because after that you won't get charged the penalty to withdrawal the money from your account, but you will be charged the additional income tax.

The reason it is important to understand the rules of borrowing from your 401(k) is because you may want to use this magical method to pay back nearly all of your debt, and you need to understand how the rules work to be able to do that. Let us say you have two cards each with $5000 on them. You just paid off the first one and are paying yourself back that debt in the form of a retirement 401(k) loan. You cannot, during the 5 years you are paying back your 401(k), borrow against the account again. You can take out the residential type of loan discussed earlier provided you have not exceeded the $50,000 in total borrowing, but you can't borrow another general purpose loan and pay off that other credit card with that $5000. As I mentioned in the rules to understand about these type accounts before though there is no penalty associated with paying back the loan early. Also, if you pay back the loan earlier than the five years you will still have to wait 60 days to borrow more money, as was mentioned above in the rules governing this type of loan. Also, that $5000 you borrowed will come out of the balance available to borrow until a full 12 months from the date of paying back the loan have transpired. Again, these are important points to consider when utilizing this method. Let us look at how we can best utilize that time.

The first time you borrow from this account you should borrow as much as you can, and transfer as much of the high interest debt to yourself as you can, because while my method will still help you pay off bank debt in the out years, it isn't as effective as the first time you do it, but it can still be very effective. Do not just borrow the minimum amount to pay off one card or one debt, but borrow as much as you can to pay off as much of your high interest debt as you can. I say high interest debt because if you have a car loan that is at 0.9% for some period of time that would not be considered a high interest loan as compared to the 6.5% investment you are losing by borrowing from your retirement account. If you do a similar comparison with what you will lose in investment interest by leaving the money in your 401(k) to what you lose in interest to this low interest car loan you will see that it would have been more financially advantageous to leave it in the retirement account and just pay back the car loan.

Five years is a long time in financial years. During that period of time you may even get a bump in the limits of your credit cards, because your score went up since the credit agencies are not reporting on that $5000 debt. If that happens, you can do some more magic to eat at even more of your debt. In other words, shift more of that debt away from a bank and instead make it work for you. I hope you follow my logic here, but let us try and use the availability of credit on the card you used to get that TV in the first place to pay back a second card that has some debt on it. That TV buying credit card may offer you, as we talked about before, low interest, or zero interest, periods to borrow more money or write convenience checks against it. Let us assume, however, they do not give you any offers, though, so we can look at the worst case. While you were making your normal contributions and paying back that retirement loan the amount of money you could borrow, up to the $50,000 maximum was going up. Again, only your contributions are available for you to borrow, so I am not talking about what your place of employment matches, but what you are contributing every other week to this account. Also not available is the amount of money you already borrowed from the account, per the rules described above, but let us be modest and assume you have another $2500 now available to you in a year from your retirement account, and another $2500 the following year. How can we use that to pay back, or transfer some of your debt to yourself; namely that other card you charged another $5000 on? After the first year you will owe about $4139 dollars still on the retirement account loan, and the following year you will owe about $3187. The first year, in my opinion, you won't have built up enough to borrow again, but the second year is a year in which we can do some damage to other high interest debts. I know you want to pay off that other debt sooner, but using your retirement account works best the first time, as I said before, then is a little less effective each time after that, unless you pay if off completely and wait the full year, because you are resetting all of the amounts available to you to borrow. In other words, doing what I am suggesting has diminishing returns as compared to the first time you do it. I also understand you will be paying the bank that interest during that two years you don't use your retirement account, but at least you can forestall a greater loss in years three through five or however long it takes you to pay off the debt through the bank. If we are now in year three, and we can borrow $3187 from our first credit card and we can use that money to immediately pay off the retirement loan, let us see if we will be better off. Doing so will start a 60 day clock that you should watch closely, because those 60 days will hurt your net gains. The debt for just those 60 days on that credit card will accrue more interest, because they will potentially charge you at a higher rate. If it is categorized as a cash advance type usage they will assign a higher interest rate. You want to limit the time you carry that balance as much as you can. In 60 days you will have a little over $5000 available to you to borrow again. This is comprised of the $2500 you contributed each of the previous two years plus two more months of contributions. Remember you can only borrow that $3187 portion after 12 months from paying it back have passed. That is why the efficacy of the method diminishes. Each paycheck you pay on the retirement loan we are using in this example will generate about 42 dollars available the next calendar year. For the sake of our example, let us say you have about $5200 dollars available to you and you will stop paying back your retirement loan since you paid it off with the credit card. If you now borrow that amount and you, first, pay off the card you charged the $3187 on less 2 months of payments to the bank you will have ($5200 − ~$3137 = $2063) available to pay down the second credit card. It is not the whole balance of $5000 you charged, but it is $2063 of that balance that can now be transferred back to you and upon which you can now make nominal returns that do not go to the bank. Two other things are important to note as well. During the 60 days you paid off the retirement loan you did not get the $84 a month deducted as repayment for the retirement loan so you can use that extra money to pay a little more to the card you borrowed the $3187 from to offset the increased interest rate. When you do go back to getting the retirement loan payments withdrawn from your pay check they are not going to be very much higher than they were before, because you are only borrowing $200 more than you did initially. In my calculations I only assumed you paid the minimum payment to the credit card for those two months ($100 a month). The new retirement loan will be about 95 dollars a month, which is still less than the minimum payment you were paying to the credit card that you now charged $5000 on. This whole process can be repeated again after some time has passed so that you build up some reserve in the retirement account. Once all of your high interest debt is transferred to your retirement account loan you will be making a little bit of money while you pay off the debt, which is certainly much better than the outright loss you suffer while you carry your debt on a credit card. Try not to get yourself into the same trouble again, but we have, after some time and some manipulating, averted disaster.

Your 401(k) general purpose loan can be used for anything you want to spend it on. It does not just have to be used on debt repayment alone. What if you did not save as much as you would have liked for your children's college expenses? Taking a loan of $50,000 from your retirement is a better option than you or your child getting into more debt, and them having to suffer the same plight you have been suffering. Similar to a debt though, you must do out the cash flow to ensure that you are not losing more than you would be if you left the money in the retirement account and took a conventional loan for college expenses. Some college expense loans come with some very low interest rates, or even deferred interest, which can give you time to pay off the loan before much interest is accrued. College loans and financing will be dealt with in a subsequent chapter, but I just don't want you to lose the hope of your children getting a college education if you were not as wise and saved when they were much younger. Let us now look at an example of how you would be better off using your retirement account to pay off a car loan that does not have a very low interest rate rather than continuing to pay the interest to a bank.

The parameters of this scenario are as follows: You borrow money to buy a car and currently have $28,400 left to pay off the car loan. The rate of the loan was 3.19% (not an unreasonable rate in today's economic environment) and the term you took on the loan was for 72 months or six years. Cars have become more expensive so in order to keep payments low financial institutions have extended the length of these loans; some even go as long as seven to eight years now. The problem with extending the loan is you end up paying more interest on the money you borrow. I am assuming, just for comparison, an annual return rate of 5% for your 401(k) account. If you have the money in your retirement account and intend to work at the place providing the retirement account for five more years then why not borrow against your retirement and pay off that car loan and instead of the bank making interest off you, you make interest off you. Again, we must look at a cash flow to see exactly what is happening:

# Financial Ninja

| | | Retirement Account | | | | | Car Loan | | |
|---|---|---|---|---|---|---|---|---|---|
| | | Payment | Principal | Interest back to you | | | Payment | Principal | Interest to the bank |
| Year 1 | 1 | 500.80 | 27952.31 | 53.11 | 0.01 | Year 1 | 1 | 434 | 28041.50 | 75.50 |
| | 2 | 500.80 | 27503.78 | 52.27 | 2.09 | | 2 | 434 | 27682.04 | 74.54 |
| | 3 | 500.80 | 27054.41 | 51.43 | 4.17 | | 3 | 434 | 27321.63 | 73.59 |
| | 4 | 500.80 | 26604.20 | 50.59 | 6.24 | | 4 | 434 | 26960.26 | 72.63 |
| | 5 | 500.80 | 26153.15 | 49.75 | 8.31 | | 5 | 434 | 26597.93 | 71.67 |
| | 6 | 500.80 | 25701.26 | 48.90 | 10.38 | | 6 | 434 | 26234.63 | 70.71 |
| | 7 | 500.80 | 25248.52 | 48.06 | 12.44 | | 7 | 434 | 25870.37 | 69.74 |
| | 8 | 500.80 | 24794.93 | 47.21 | 14.50 | | 8 | 434 | 25505.15 | 68.77 |
| | 9 | 500.80 | 24340.50 | 46.37 | 16.56 | | 9 | 434 | 25138.95 | 67.80 |
| | 10 | 500.80 | 23885.22 | 45.52 | 18.61 | | 10 | 434 | 24771.77 | 66.83 |
| | 11 | 500.80 | 23429.08 | 44.66 | 20.66 | | 11 | 434 | 24403.63 | 65.85 |
| | 12 | 500.80 | 22972.10 | 43.81 | 22.70 | | 12 | 434 | 24034.50 | 64.87 |
| Year 2 | 1 | 500.80 | 22514.25 | 42.96 | 24.74 | Year 2 | 1 | 434 | 23664.39 | 63.89 |
| | 2 | 500.80 | 22055.56 | 42.10 | 26.78 | | 2 | 434 | 23293.30 | 62.91 |
| | 3 | 500.80 | 21596.00 | 41.24 | 28.81 | | 3 | 434 | 22921.22 | 61.92 |
| | 4 | 500.80 | 21135.58 | 40.38 | 30.84 | | 4 | 434 | 22548.15 | 60.93 |
| | 5 | 500.80 | 20674.31 | 39.52 | 32.86 | | 5 | 434 | 22174.09 | 59.94 |
| | 6 | 500.80 | 20212.17 | 38.66 | 34.88 | | 6 | 434 | 21799.04 | 58.95 |
| | 7 | 500.80 | 19749.17 | 37.80 | 36.90 | | 7 | 434 | 21422.99 | 57.95 |
| | 8 | 500.80 | 19285.30 | 36.93 | 38.92 | | 8 | 434 | 21045.94 | 56.95 |
| | 9 | 500.80 | 18820.56 | 36.06 | 40.93 | | 9 | 434 | 20667.88 | 55.95 |
| | 10 | 500.80 | 18354.95 | 35.19 | 42.93 | | 10 | 434 | 20288.83 | 54.94 |
| | 11 | 500.80 | 17888.48 | 34.32 | 44.93 | | 11 | 434 | 19908.76 | 53.93 |
| | 12 | 500.80 | 17421.13 | 33.45 | 46.93 | | 12 | 434 | 19527.68 | 52.92 |
| Year 3 | 1 | 500.80 | 16952.91 | 32.58 | 48.93 | Year 3 | 1 | 434 | 19145.60 | 51.91 |
| | 2 | 500.80 | 16483.81 | 31.70 | 50.92 | | 2 | 434 | 18762.49 | 50.90 |
| | 3 | 500.80 | 16013.83 | 30.82 | 52.91 | | 3 | 434 | 18378.37 | 49.88 |
| | 4 | 500.80 | 15542.98 | 29.95 | 54.89 | | 4 | 434 | 17993.22 | 48.86 |
| | 5 | 500.80 | 15071.24 | 29.07 | 56.87 | | 5 | 434 | 17607.05 | 47.83 |
| | 6 | 500.80 | 14598.63 | 28.18 | 58.85 | | 6 | 434 | 17219.86 | 46.81 |
| | 7 | 500.80 | 14125.13 | 27.30 | 60.82 | | 7 | 434 | 16831.64 | 45.78 |
| | 8 | 500.80 | 13650.74 | 26.41 | 62.79 | | 8 | 434 | 16442.38 | 44.74 |
| | 9 | 500.80 | 13175.47 | 25.53 | 64.75 | | 9 | 434 | 16052.09 | 43.71 |
| | 10 | 500.80 | 12699.31 | 24.64 | 66.71 | | 10 | 434 | 15660.76 | 42.67 |
| | 11 | 500.80 | 12222.25 | 23.75 | 68.67 | | 11 | 434 | 15268.39 | 41.63 |
| | 12 | 500.80 | 11744.31 | 22.86 | 70.63 | | 12 | 434 | 14874.98 | 40.59 |
| Year 4 | 1 | 500.80 | 11265.47 | 21.96 | 72.58 | Year 4 | 1 | 434 | 14480.52 | 39.54 |
| | 2 | 500.80 | 10785.74 | 21.07 | 74.52 | | 2 | 434 | 14085.02 | 38.49 |
| | 3 | 500.80 | 10305.11 | 20.17 | 76.47 | | 3 | 434 | 13688.46 | 37.44 |
| | 4 | 500.80 | 9823.58 | 19.27 | 78.41 | | 4 | 434 | 13290.85 | 36.39 |
| | 5 | 500.80 | 9341.15 | 18.37 | 80.34 | | 5 | 434 | 12892.18 | 35.33 |
| | 6 | 500.80 | 8857.82 | 17.47 | 82.28 | | 6 | 434 | 12492.45 | 34.27 |
| | 7 | 500.80 | 8373.58 | 16.56 | 84.20 | | 7 | 434 | 12091.66 | 33.21 |
| | 8 | 500.80 | 7888.44 | 15.66 | 86.13 | | 8 | 434 | 11689.80 | 32.14 |
| | 9 | 500.80 | 7402.39 | 14.75 | 88.05 | | 9 | 434 | 11286.88 | 31.08 |
| | 10 | 500.80 | 6915.43 | 13.84 | 89.97 | | 10 | 434 | 10882.88 | 30.00 |
| | 11 | 500.80 | 6427.56 | 12.93 | 91.88 | | 11 | 434 | 10477.81 | 28.93 |
| | 12 | 500.80 | 5938.78 | 12.02 | 93.79 | | 12 | 434 | 10071.67 | 27.85 |
| Year 5 | 1 | 500.80 | 5449.09 | 11.11 | 95.70 | Year 5 | 1 | 434 | 9664.44 | 26.77 |
| | 2 | 500.80 | 4958.48 | 10.19 | 97.61 | | 2 | 434 | 9256.13 | 25.69 |
| | 3 | 500.80 | 4466.95 | 9.27 | 99.51 | | 3 | 434 | 8846.74 | 24.61 |
| | 4 | 500.80 | 3974.51 | 8.35 | 101.40 | | 4 | 434 | 8436.26 | 23.52 |
| | 5 | 500.80 | 3481.14 | 7.43 | 103.39 | | 5 | 434 | 8024.68 | 22.43 |
| | 6 | 500.80 | 2986.85 | 6.51 | 105.19 | | 6 | 434 | 7612.02 | 21.33 |
| | 7 | 500.80 | 2491.63 | 5.59 | 107.07 | | 7 | 434 | 7198.25 | 20.24 |
| | 8 | 500.80 | 1995.49 | 4.66 | 108.95 | | 8 | 434 | 6783.37 | 19.14 |
| | 9 | 500.80 | 1498.42 | 3.73 | 110.83 | | 9 | 434 | 6367.42 | 18.03 |
| | 10 | 500.80 | 1000.43 | 2.80 | 112.71 | | 10 | 434 | 5950.35 | 16.93 |
| | 11 | 500.80 | 501.45 | 1.87 | 114.58 | | 11 | 434 | 5532.16 | 15.82 |
| | 12 | 500.80 | 1.63 | 0.94 | 116.45 | | 12 | 434 | 5112.87 | 14.71 |
| | | | | $1649.60 | $3556.87 | Year 6 | 1 | 434 | 4692.46 | 13.59 |
| | | | | | | | 2 | 434 | 4270.94 | 12.47 |
| | | | | | | | 3 | 434 | 3848.29 | 11.35 |
| | | | | | | | 4 | 434 | 3424.52 | 10.23 |
| | | | | | | | 5 | 434 | 2999.62 | 9.10 |
| | | | | | | | 6 | 434 | 2573.60 | 7.97 |
| | | | | | | | 7 | 434 | 2146.44 | 6.84 |
| | | | | | | | 8 | 434 | 1718.14 | 5.71 |
| | | | | | | | 9 | 434 | 1288.71 | 4.57 |
| | | | | | | | 10 | 434 | 858.14 | 3.43 |
| | | | | | | | 11 | 434 | 426.42 | 2.28 |
| | | | | | | | 12 | 434 | ≈0 | 1.13 |
| | | | | | | | | | | $2841.55 |

Jason Evans

I have compared the two loans side by side so that you can see what you pay or make each month on the two different loans. First, as you can see, the retirement loan has slightly higher payments, but that is because you are paying it off in five years since that is the maximum length you can carry a loan from your retirement account. The car loan is amortized over six years through the bank so $434 is your monthly payment to execute that loan. The bottom line numbers are important for comparison. The retirement loan shows you what you will pay back to yourself for borrowing money from this account (the 3$^{rd}$ column), but you are also making the 5% annual rate of return on money you are putting back into the account (that is the 4$^{th}$ column of numbers). Now how much would you make if you just left the money in the retirement account with an annual rate of return for six years:

| | |
|---|---|
| Year 1 | $28400.00 |
| Year 2 | $29820.00 |
| Year 3 | $31311.00 |
| Year 4 | $32876.55 |
| Year 5 | $34520.38 |
| Year 6 | $36246.40 |

That would give you about ($36,246.40-$28,400.00) or $7846.40 of growth during the same six years you are paying back the car loan. The problem is you don't make, in the aggregate, that return, because you must take out all of that interest you paid to the bank. So you, really, make ($7846.40-$2841.55) or $5004.85. That is your effective return comparing the retirement account growing and the car loan going down. So what about the option of using your retirement account to pay off the car loan? What is your effective return then? It is the sum of the two numbers at the bottom of the retirement account cash flow PLUS the interest you will now make on the full amount for year six, since you paid off that loan a year early. In other words, ($1649.60 + $3556.87 + $1420) or $6626.47, but they will charge you a fee of about $50 dollars to take out this loan as you recall from before, so you really make $6576.47. Comparing the three scenarios, obviously, leaving the money in makes the highest return, but we need to look in the aggregate. Once you include the loan that you pay separately leaving that money in your 401(k) account nets you only $5004.85 over the six years. That is less than $6576.47 by $1571.62. Yes, clearly you made less than if you left it in the retirement account, but the reality is you also have that pesky car loan which erodes those clean returns. It is better to take the loan from your retirement account, pay off that car loan, and then pay yourself back. You make $1571.62 more. Let us not forget the ancillary benefit of not having the car loan reported on your credit report anymore the day you pay it off either. That will help your credit score while you are paying yourself back. Not bad, in my opinion, and you still get to drive around in your new car.

I am sure your financial advisor would caution you here too, but these retirement loans can be used for business ventures as well. Just remember, if you do decide to open a business with a loan from your own retirement, you run a slightly higher risk since the business could fail and you could then be simply paying back a loan to yourself for that failed business. If you have a solid business plan, and your only impediment is a little bit of seed money then a loan from your retirement account may be better than a small business loan or even a venture capitalist who ends up forcing you into terms that make them money, and leave you with very little.

Some words of caution though regarding the retirement account method of debt reduction. While you are making a little bit of money still in the aggregate, you were not, and will not making as much money as the person who didn't touch their retirement and did not charge the $5000 TV. So I am not advocating excessive spending and then paying back those loans with your retirement. Also, if you are closer than five years to retirement, it becomes more advantageous to leave your money in your retirement to work for you. You don't want to rob your retirement account right before you are going to be taking distributions from it to live on. Also, unless you have a very significant financially devastated situation or incur a medical condition which requires more money than you have, I would strongly caution you from taking a withdrawal (not the loans we have been talking about) from your retirement account, because of both the penalty you will take as well as the income tax bill you will incur from that type of withdrawal. The account is designed to help you weather the years you are not working, and withdrawals do not allow you to do that. They burn that money and any potential investment interest gains as well. It just is not worth it.

We have seen in this chapter that just because you got yourself into some financial trouble all hope was not lost. A home and a job with a retirement account can be more than just a place to stay and something to help you live a certain lifestyle when you do finally stop working. So now let us look at how we can build up our retirement for either debt reduction or to use in our golden years.

## CHAPTER 4—RETIREMENT

*My parents, like so many Americans, planned for retirement by working, and hoping Social Security would cover their expenses in retirement. My father worked and got a pension from his place of employment, but having earned very little over his lifetime his benefits for both the pension and his contributions to Social Security didn't amount to enough to sustain himself. His lack of skills filled in the holes to ensure he would be completely unprepared to actually stop working. On paper he is retired, but he continues to fill jobs that require less and less skill to accomplish. No offense to the* people performing the job of packing Amazon shipping boxes, but this is one of the thankless, and unrewarding, jobs he was forced to fill. It turns out, Amazon feels this job could be filled by a robot, because the error rate they allow is some ridiculously small amount that no human, at least not at the rate they are packing boxes at Amazon, could ever hope to achieve so, naturally, turnover is very high. Around the same time my father was working for Amazon I received a shipment from Amazon that was improperly filled. I couldn't help but think it had been packed by my father, who, interestingly, wasn't employed at Amazon shortly after my package arrived, and I informed Amazon that it had been filled incorrectly. I am being glib, but it is sad that he worked most of his adult life, served in the military, and yet, still, has nothing to sustain himself with when he is unable to work as he once did.

My mother didn't prepare either, well, perhaps she did, but not in the traditional manner. She seems to get more and more pets as she gets older. Maybe she is doing this in the hope of having a food source available should her meager funds from Social Security fail to cover her food bills. I don't have the heart to tell her that maintaining the stable of pets is likely to outweigh the four little meals they may provide should worse come to worst. She, too, worked most of her life, but, like many Americans, just assumed Social Security would prepare her for retired life. She does watch an incredible amount of television, and I am here to tell you, despite what others may tell you, the advice being passed out on these self-help television shows has clearly not rubbed off on her. The pets seem to have a pretty good retired life, though. They don't even eat bagged and processed dog or cat food. They are prepared meals each day with items similar to what you and I eat, and even have spots on the dining table from which to eat these feasts. This is not so good when you are a neat-freak like myself and visit and are offered "cold cuts" as a snack prepared, and placed, on this same table. I once politely partook of the food being offered and soon found myself coughing up my own hairball. She also tells me that the TV must be left on even when she is not there because the animals watch it. Perhaps they are the ones picking up on *the advice being dispensed, and why they are living the retired life that my mother had envisioned for herself.*

Most people will tell you to plan early for retirement. Some will even explain in more detail why you should start early, namely because of what is known as: *the time value of money*. The sooner you start earning interest the greater amount of money you will have in the out years. What they neglect to tell you is what you should be investing in so that you are adequately prepared for that period of time when you are not working. They also make no mention of the balance you must strike between current living conditions, paying debt, and saving for retirement. It doesn't pay, for example, to save for retirement early when you have credit cards that are burning 18 to 19% of your income, annually. Also, conventional wisdom, to which I do not subscribe, is to invest in more risky things at a younger age, and invest in less risky things as you get older. As with most of the things I have discussed in this book, my suggestions flout many of these conventions, as you shall see.

My advice is age independent, which means you should be doing similar things regardless of your age, and it is backed by sound financial logic, which is something you should always look for when receiving financial advice. If someone, myself included, tells you something that sounds very good, then I would first check its numbers, because in the financial world if such good deals really existed the market would have already found it, and would have eroded any significant gains well before you get your hands on it. That having been said, here now is my advice for you to verify.

First, when you should start savings is as soon as you can. This aspect of traditional financial wisdom is something with which I agree. This isn't a new concept, I think most people already know this, but they talk themselves out of it because they believe it would be better to pay off school loans or some other debts they got before their current job. Even with the credit card debts we talked about in previous chapters, you can still save. You just may be saving less than you would otherwise. Also, they may think 10% to 15% of their income would make too much of a dent in their current style of living. I doubt that with your first job you will be offered some sort of retirement package, or opportunity, but, at some point, if your job offers you an opportunity to save for your retirement, in the form of a 401(k), you should do it, even if it hurts a little. By hurting a little, I mean if your place of employment offers any matching whatsoever you should, at least, invest to that point, as I will show you in a minute. It is important to understand why it is a good idea to save to that maximum matching amount. If your employer offers 5% matching, for example, and you only invest 2% then you are effectively giving up an additional 3% of free money. Some numbers will help to demonstrate what you are giving up, and I do mean giving up:

| Your pay | Year | What it will grow to at 2% | What it will grow to if you put in the max of 5% |
| --- | --- | --- | --- |
| $30,000.00 | 1 | $1,235.26 | $3,088.16 |
| $30,000.00 | 2 | $2,546.82 | $6,367.05 |
| $30,000.00 | 3 | $3,939.38 | $9,848.46 |
| $30,000.00 | 4 | $5,417.95 | $13,544.89 |
| $30,000.00 | 5 | $6,987.85 | $17,469.62 |
| $30,000.00 | 6 | $8,654.70 | $21,636.75 |
| $30,000.00 | 7 | $10,424.51 | $26,061.27 |
| $30,000.00 | 8 | $12,303.62 | $30,759.05 |
| $30,000.00 | 9 | $14,298.79 | $35,746.98 |
| $30,000.00 | 10 | $16,417.19 | $41,042.99 |

As you can see, what you are giving up is quite significant, if you don't chose to invest to the maximum matching amount. What is happening here is that your 2% is being matched so you are investing 4%, and that 4% is earning interest as you both invest each paycheck (about $23 of yours and $23 of your employer's assets) and as it earns interest as an investment to the totals shown here. In the 5% matching scenario the same thing is happening, just with more money. You are investing about $57 dollars per paycheck, but your employer is doing the same thing on your behalf. You are investing more, but your employer is also matching more. The "more" you are investing is only the difference between the $23 you were investing per paycheck and the $57 you are investing per paycheck in the higher matching scenario. That difference is only $34 per paycheck, but that amount is being matched, and as you can see that small change has a big big effect on your overall investment. I only assumed a modest 6% investment growth rate as an investment rate, but regardless of the rate you get, unless, of course, you actually get negative returns, your money will grow faster as you put in more, and also, because your employer is matching that greater amount. That matching is free money. This is a static situation too, it does not assume you get any raises, which if you did get, during the ten years would make both go up. The spread between the two growth amounts would become even greater. In other words, there is no normal situation in which it would be a good idea to not take the free money and invest it. Certainly, if you have sick relative or some other dire financial situation you may choose to alleviate that situation before saving for retirement, just understand the consequences of doing so. Also, as I outlined in the previous chapter regarding a very effective way of prosecuting debt, you could borrow a lot more from the retirement account to pay off debts you accrued during the ten years. For example, at year seven, from above, what is available to borrow on the 2% table is, maybe, $4000, while on the 5% table, you could borrow closer to between $11,000 and $12,000. Do not forget that if you should borrow from that, now, more robust, retirement account, you will be paying yourself back, and not a bank.

Should you put more money in than what your employer matches? The answer to this is yes, if you can. Any money you can put in this account will only help it grow, but this is where you may want to execute your credit card debt instead of saving more for your retirement, but again, saving more will only make it grow more. There are limits to how much you can contribute, or save in a tax deferred manner, though. In 2017, that yearly amount was

$18,000 that you could contribute, not including what your employer matches. In 2018, that amount is set to go up to $18,500. If you are over 50, you can contribute an additional $6,000 a year in what is known as "catch-up" contributions. The overall limit that can be contributed to a 401(k) was $54,000 in 2017. In 2018, this overall maximum is set to go up to $55,000. If you are over 50 the $6,000 catch-up money is added to these total amounts for a maximum of $60,000 for 2017, and $61,000 for 2018. These same kinds of limits apply to the other retirement account flavors like: 403(b) and 457(b)s. The reason the overall limits are higher is because your employer can contribute up to 25% of your compensation. Some of which may, or may not, be matching type contributions. Whatever your employer's maximum matching is, that is, at least, what you should contribute, and if they put more in on your behalf, that only helps you. Most financial planners will suggest you put about 10% to 15% of your annual salary into retirement savings. That includes the matching you would get from your employer. I think 15% is a little high, because that number is based on a lower return rate on your investment than I think you will get, at least, historically speaking. If your employer matches 5% and you put in 5% that makes your total 10% overall, but don't forget there are other investments you could be making that would add to this 10%. If you have some other investment vehicle that too should be included in that overall percentage calculation to determine how much you are saving for retirement. What you should be investing your money in is nearly as important as investing at all.

As I said before, my advice is age agnostic. The only thing that I think may change as you advance in years is the overall percentage of what you invest in each category. Your retirement account is not something with which you should really play. You should try to put money in it and leave it there. That does not include the loans I talked about before. What I mean is, it does not serve you well to shift your money around too often, or change the underlying vehicle that the money is pinned to. The largest portion of your retirement account should be in something that gives good returns, and is modestly safe.

Safety of money is an important discussion point though, and so we should address it now.

I often hear people say their money is in a safe investment, because it is in something other than common stocks or index funds that are not made up of common stocks. They tell me that it is safe because it will maintain its value. I find this logic flawed in that, to me, safety is the money value itself. The more you have the safer you are. I am comfortable with my money fluctuating over time, so long as at the time I need to use it that pot is as large as it can be. Another example is helpful to see what I mean. Here is that same retirement account that you started when you starting working, but now at an investment rate of return of 3%:

| Your pay | Year | What it will grow to at 2% | What it will grow to if you put in the max of 5% |
| --- | --- | --- | --- |
| $30,000.00 | 1 | $1,217.47 | $3,043.67 |
| $30,000.00 | 2 | $2,471.99 | $6,179.98 |
| $30,000.00 | 3 | $3,764.70 | $9,411.75 |
| $30,000.00 | 4 | $5,096.75 | $12,741.89 |
| $30,000.00 | 5 | $6,672.26 | $16,680.66 |
| $30,000.00 | 6 | $8,295.72 | $20,739.31 |
| $30,000.00 | 7 | $9,968.60 | $24,921.50 |
| $30,000.00 | 8 | $11,692.39 | $29,230.98 |
| $30,000.00 | 9 | $13,468.65 | $33,671.62 |
| $30,000.00 | 10 | $15,298.97 | $38,247.42 |

Let us assume, you invested the maximum we talked about before of 5% with 5% matching. Your money grew to only $38,247.42 as opposed to $41,042.99 in a 6% rate ofreturn growth environment. That is $2,795.57 less in ten years. To me that extra $2,795.57 is more safety than would be possible in the lower amount scenario even if that scenario didn't have as many perturbations over the course of ten years. What these people are forgetting about is *average* annual returns. Average returns are what I call safety. If my average annual returns are higher than yours I am safer than you are, because I will make more money over the same period of time. Who cares, ok perhaps you care a little, but if one year my fund makes a -5% return while you were making +2% returns in your safe investment. Yes, your investment will beat mine that one year, maybe, but if the following year mine goes up to +10% and yours goes up to +2.5% then over the course of the two years I beat you, *on average*. My net gain over the 2 years was $\frac{-5+10}{2} = 2.5\%$ yours was $\frac{2+2.5}{2} = 2.25\%$. The average returns over a period of time are what you should be focusing on when you decide where you want to put your money for retirement.

Here is an interesting fact that was demonstrated to me with regard to average annual returns, and was an eye-opener for me. The average annual return of the *Standard & Poor 500* (S&P 500) Index fund, since inception, in 1928, has been, after you adjust for inflation, about 7%. That means it has outperformed your safer investments for almost a century, on average. That does not mean you should expect to get returns quite that high, hence my using 6% instead of 7%. Also, there were periods, long periods, of poor returns throughout the index fund's history. That doesn't mean it is not a good investment for your retirement money. Even Warren Buffet was quoted as saying something to the effect of leave your money in a S&P fund and let industry do its work. An index fund, in case you are interest, is a fund that is comprised of a mixed flavor of the market assets upon which the fund is based. The *Standard and Poor 500* is comprised of a mix of 500 companies shares represented on several trading forums. It is mix of mostly larger capitalized companies and has become, perhaps arguably, the industry standard upon which the overall health of the financial market as a whole is benchmarked. The old benchmark was the *Dow Jones Industrial Average* (DJIA), which is comprised of 30 companies traded on the New York Stock Exchange (NYSE). These two are the two acronyms you see as having gone up or down on most market news outlets. You have probably have seen them, but may not have known what they represented. The DJIA has been shortened to DOW and the *S&P 500* to S&P. The other overall market barometer is the National Association of Securities Dealers Automated Quotations (NASDAQ). This one just represents the activity on that exchange. The DOW has become atavistic in my opinion since it only tracks 30 companies on the NYSE. It worked fine in the early 20$^{th}$ century when there was not the veritable plethora of companies that are now being traded upon commercially. This brings me to my first suggestion for where you should put most of your money for retirement.

If you put 60% of your money early on in an S&P 500 index fund you would be, in my humble opinion, putting your money in a safe investment, from an earnings perspective. There are other, newer, and perhaps sexier, index funds out there, like the *Russell 2000*, as well as several offerings of both Fidelity and Vanguard. Your company will likely have, at least, one market index pinned retirement offering and that is where you should put the moiety of your money. Another important advantage of index funds is that their fees, or costs associated with the account, will be less than a more closely managed fund so more of your retirement money will be going to work for you. Do look at the fees associated with any retirement account fund you decide to invest in, though. Some charge very high fees because the managers of that fund are constantly trying to beat the market, and so shift money around frequently. They can often times beat the market, but you are looking for long term growth for this fund, not short-term, potentially unsustainable, growth. That is what the other 40% of your retirement account is designed to accommodate. If you put another 20% into something that invests in what is known as a small-cap fund, or a fund made up of companies with smaller capitalization rates (essentially the size of the company), you would be investing in something safe yet not as safe as a S&P backed fund. The last 20% can be put into internationally backed funds or just about anything you see has having decent sustained average returns, and a fee that is not higher than 2 to 3%. It can even be invested directly into a particular company's common stock, if you so choose. That should round out the full 100% of your investment dollars. International funds tend to have opposite growth to the U.S. market so they can be seen as hedges. A hedge is anything that is designed to protect against the underlying investments risk. Banks have all kinds of hedge mechanism to cover investments in futures or currency so why shouldn't you, at least, attempt a distilled version of this method.

The only thing that could change over time is the mix of these three components of your retirement account. As you get older you can shift away from the smaller capitalization and the last 20% as play money and, instead, invest more in index pinned funds that are more closely aligned with the *S&P 500*. Closer to an 80/20 mix rather than 60/40, or if you are really risk averse, invest only in the *S&P 500* index fund closer to your retirement, but do not put it in very low rate of return type investments as you approach retirement.

IRAs are another form of deferred savings. There are traditional IRA where you contribute tax free, and at withdrawal time, are then taxed on the withdrawals you make. There are also Roth IRAs that allow you to contribute money that you still pay taxes on now, but at the time you make withdrawals, provided you meet the age requirement, those withdrawals are tax free at that time. An important note is that you can contribute to BOTH your 401(k) as well as either a traditional or Roth IRA at the same time. The maximum amount, currently, you can contribute to any combination of traditional IRA or Roth IRA is $5,500 or $6,500 if you are over 50. The mixture can be either all traditional or all Roth or a combination of the two, but your overall contribution cannot be more than the maximums listed above. The reason I bring it up, though, is because if you still have some disposable cash after you are contributing the maximum amount to your 401(k) then these two options allow you to make that leftover money work for you now. An extra $5,500 each year will add up to even more money by the time you choose to use it for retirement.

    The biggest mistake I see people who retire making while they are not retired is thinking they should either: move all of their money to a more secure fund backed by government treasury bonds, or move it to something "safer" with a low return, but one that has maintained that return over a long long period of time. People mistakenly define being risk averse as needing to put your money in something "safe" to preserve it. We talked about this before, but it bears repeating. Money, to me, is security, not the security of the fund itself. The best analogy I can use to describe what is happening to your money at retirement and why you should still keep your money in something like a *S&P 500* index fund is a bathtub in which water is being both added, and water is being removed. If you turn on the faucet and add water to the tub it will overflow with interest returns, which is what you hope to have happen in the years leading up to your retirement. At retirement though, water is added to this tub at a slower rate, but simultaneously water is also being removed from this bathtub. Now the water will not overflow because you are using part of this bathtub of water to sustain your lifestyle. If you use too much of the water, the water going in will not be able to keep up, but the point of the bathtub at retirement is to use too much or to, at least, break even. It is your money that you want to now play with and take vacations you put off or, at least, use to maintain the same level of income you had while you were working. The *S&P 500* Index fund faucet is putting water in the tub at an average annual rate of around 6% while you are simultaneously drawing a constant amount of water out, but if you switch your money over to a fund earning a more secure flow of water in at 2%, while you are still drawing a constant amount of water out of the bathtub, your bathtub will start going down at a rate faster than my bathtub. Again, the security to me is earning more money on my money while I am removing money or building up my retirement account, not securely maintaining an account that I am drawing a constant amount of water from—only at a lower "safer" rate of return. Leave your money in the account making a constant average return of 6%. You may say, but what about those years the fund goes down -30% and then back up +35% the following year. Those years, too, you should leave your money in the index fund, because you are still withdrawing a constant amount from the account. The only time you would care what the annual returns are is in any year you choose to liquidate more than your annual withdrawal to maintain your lifestyle. Maybe you want to pay off your house or, maybe, you want to buy a home for your children. Then, and only in that year will you want to, wait until the returns are on the upswing and not the downswing, because you are seriously denting your account. If you do something like this, though, also realize the income tax ramifications. The IRS still takes money from you when you are retired, and so they would very much love for you to take out a lump sum of $250,000 from your retirement account, because then they will charge you income tax at a higher rate than you were enjoying at constant annual withdrawals—after all, you had a big plus up one year. You are getting taxed on whatever you normally take out plus the extra amount because, for that tax year, your income went up—substantially. Another point to consider is: should you move money from one account to another while you are building it up?

The answer to this question is it depends on what you are moving the money from and what you are moving it to. Once you are investing in a retirement fund, of any kind, you are, essentially, trading just like if you had bought common stocks. The reason why you see a share price on your account is because it is the only way they can normalize all investors in that fund who do not put the same amount of money in their accounts. That share price is the rate at which biweekly paycheck investment buy into the investment account. It allows for any amount of money you put into the account to be accommodated. If you put in 50 dollars every two weeks, and the fund required you to have 75 dollars before you can buy one share, then you would not be able to put any money in the first paycheck, and you would only have one share by the second paycheck. Instead, they allow you to buy a portion of the share with your $50 on both, the first, and second, paycheck allowing you to own 1.33 by your second paycheck. This is the power of any fund. You do not have to buy a whole of any of the shares. Those shares, though, now have a fluctuating value just like common stocks do. If you want to shift your money, you have to sell whatever portion you want to move at the value that day, and buy the new fund at its share price on that day. Most company funds, at least those following the U.S. Department of Labor's guidelines for mutual funds, should allow you to shift your money around quarterly. Your employer must tell you how often you can do this, and it is more often than not almost a zero sum game. There are instances where you could lose a little money in the shift, because, after all, the reason you are likely moving the money is because your current fund is underperforming and you would like to get the annual returns of another fund that is performing better. If the fund you are looking to sell is doing very poorly that day, and the fund you are looking to shift it to is doing very well that day, you will lose some value overall in the shift. The next day though you will start making money at the new, hopefully higher, rate, and that is good news. If you are moving money around, just try to do it when the two funds are closer in value or, at least, their value has normalized or accept that you may lose a little money in the short-run. If you are in fact investing in a fund that has higher returns than the fund your money was in before, the money you make in the long-run should outweigh this short term loss.

Inflation is something that financial planners will, at least, make you consider, but in my opinion inflation is akin to a sunk cost. It isn't something you can prevent yourself. You cannot protect yourself from erosion of your money due to inflation in the same way you cannot prevent erosion by not investing in a higher, more "risky", average annual return rate investment. Simply do not do it. Keep your money in accounts that earn higher average annual returns so that your money builds up faster, regardless of inflation, over time. It should grow to a greater amount then when you started and drawing from it, at whatever the prevailing inflation rate is at the time you retire, you will still have money to live off of in your retirement years. Just like the scenario, described above, in which you chose to shift your money to an investment backed in more secure investments, but only earned 2% on your money, while the average annual inflation rate was 3%, you are still, technically speaking, losing money each year. You are losing less money than if you had stuffed it in your mattress, but you are losing money, none the less. If you, instead, are making an average annual return of 6.5% while inflation is 3% you are in fact making money each year. I cannot stress enough the safety of putting your money in a place where it makes greater average annual returns. This greater amount of money will, as it should, provide you more safety than preserving a smaller amount of money. Investing in higher annual rate of return investments protect you from inflation, erosion of your funds, and provides you the real security you are after.

Social security is another important point to consider when devising a retirement portfolio. Few people really understand how social security works, and there is plenty of advice floating around about what you should, and should not, do. Predicting just how much you will have available to you when you do decide to retire is not a very straightforward question either. The Social Security administration sends you a yearly statement that will give you a rough estimate of how much you will get at 62 and your full retirement age. How they calculate this amount is a fairly complex calculation that involves the number of what they consider "qualifying months" of work. They also take the top 35 years of your employment time to come up with an average salary from which your benefits are calculated. If you have a spotty work history, it makes that number lower. It is easiest to calculate if you have a constantly growing salary over the years, but many of us do not have such a history. It can also be harder to calculate both you and your spouse's exact amount if one of you doesn't work, while the other does, for any extended period of time. The more time you do not work, the less overall benefit you will get. Also, the more you make, up to a limit, will, generally, give you a greater benefit. The government is also constantly tinkering with this entitlement (although I use that term loosely since it is not really a true entitlement) to keep it afloat. For people my age, and younger, I am not entirely certain it will even be available at all when we reach retirement age. The point at which you get full retirement also depends on your age, and it is likely that age will continue to climb as people, on average, are living longer. Currently, if you are born before 1959 you can receive full retirement benefits at age 66. If you are born after 1959 then you have to wait another year, and are 67. Also, the convoluted requirements to file and suspend your social security benefits have expired. Even as I write this, I expect some of the things I am telling you to change. As I mentioned before, there is a maximum benefit you can draw as well, regardless of how much you have worked, or made, over the history of your working years. People do not understand that there is a maximum amount that social security will pay you, even though the amount you put into it could be more. That maximum benefit is, currently, $31,956 per year at full retirement. If you choose to start collecting at 62, which is the first year you are eligible to receive social security, then you could only get 70% of the amount you would have gotten at full retirement age. If you wait to start collecting until you are 70, you could get 24% more than what you could get at full retirement age, if you were born after 1959, and as much as 32.5% more, if you were born before 1959. Without describing the file and suspend rules, and only frustrating you that they no longer exist, what is the right age to start collecting. People have their own opinions about the right age to collect, and I will not tell you they are wrong. I will try to fully paint some possible scenarios, and explain the impact of each to your retirement portfolio, and let you make your own decision. It is my hope that you will try to get to the earliest point you can stop working, because you have worked hard to get to retirement age, and I would prefer you enjoy it younger than working yourself, literally, to death. There are plenty of people I see saying they will stop working when they are 70, and are almost forced to retire, but these same people suffer a debilitating illness, or worse die, before they even get to enjoy their golden years. Money is a tool not unlike any other tool. Get to the point where you are comfortable, and not a day later, because as we age we can predict with less and less certainty that we will be healthy or otherwise able to enjoy the period of time we are no longer working. In order to see these pictures I will draw, we need to look at the cash flow of each scenario. Again, cash flow, at least for me, shows me the effects of any investment scenario much better than some person pontificating about the merits of their plan. For the sake of simplicity, we will use 62, 67, and 70 and assume you have invested enough to get the maximum amount of Social Security benefit available from your work history:

# Financial Ninja

| 62 Monthly | | 67 Monthly | | 70 Monthly | |
|---|---|---|---|---|---|
| 1997.25 | | 2663.00 | | 3302.12 | |
| 62 | 23967 | 62 | | 62 | |
| 63 | 23967 | 63 | | 63 | |
| 64 | 23967 | 64 | | 64 | |
| 65 | 23967 | 65 | | 65 | |
| 66 | 23967 | 66 | | 66 | |
| 67 | 23967 | 67 | 31956 | 67 | |
| 68 | 23967 | 68 | 31956 | 68 | |
| 69 | 23967 | 69 | 31956 | 69 | |
| 70 | 23967 | 70 | 31956 | 70 | 39625 |
| 71 | 23967 | 71 | 31956 | 71 | 39625 |
| 72 | 23967 | 72 | 31956 | 72 | 39625 |
| 73 | 23967 | 73 | 31956 | 73 | 39625 |
| 74 | 23967 | 74 | 31956 | 74 | 39625 |
| 75 | 23967 | 75 | 31956 | 75 | 39625 |
| 76 | 23967 | 76 | 31956 | 76 | 39625 |
| 77 | 23967 | 77 | 31956 | 77 | 39625 |
| 78 | 23967 | 78 | 31956 | 78 | 39625 |
| 79 | 23967 | 79 | 31956 | 79 | 39625 |
| 80 | 23967 | 80 | 31956 | 80 | 39625 |
| 81 | 23967 | 81 | 31956 | 81 | 39625 |
| 82 | 23967 | 82 | 31956 | 82 | 39625 |
| 83 | 23967 | 83 | 31956 | 83 | 39625 |
| 84 | 23967 | 84 | 31956 | 84 | 39625 |
| 85 | 23967 | 85 | 31956 | 85 | 39625 |
| 86 | 23967 | 86 | 31956 | 86 | 39625 |
| Total | $599,175.00 | Total | $639,120.00 | Total | $673,632.48 |

The amounts are the thing you should focus on in these cash flows. This shows how much you will make before taxes over a similar period of time. It allows you to compare apples to apples. The difference between 62 and 70 is about $73,000. That is a lot of money, so you should wait to collect then shouldn't you? The answer, to me though, is a resounding no. That may seem like a lot of money, but it is not when you consider what you have to do during the period of time *before* you start receiving these higher benefits. What do you live on from 62 until 70? The reason I didn't refer to you retiring and instead said "receive benefits" is because when you actually stop working, and when you receive benefits are independent ideas. My assumptions do conclude that you will not continue working during the period of time you are retiring and are seeing these social security cash flows. If you do choose to work then, obviously, that is what you will live on, but what if you do actually follow my plan and use that time to enjoy a period of time when you do not work?

If you do decide to continue working understand that the government has rules for doing that as well. In 2017, the limit on how much you can earn, and still collect full retirement (full meaning whatever you should be getting at whatever age you retire), is $16,920. If you earn more than this then for every two dollars over that amount they will reduce your benefit by one dollar. This all assumes you are not at *full* retirement age. In the year you reach full retirement age, they change the rules a little and take only one dollar for every three dollars you earn. The earnings are only for those months before you reach full retirement age. So if you are in your 67$^{th}$ year and your birthday is in June then they would only use those months before June to calculate if you had gone over the limit. In 2017, the overall limit was $44,880, which equates to $3740 per month that you could earn and, for which, they will take out only one dollar for every three over that monthly limit. Obviously, only someone born on the very last day of the year or, at least, very near it would be affected by such a limit. Once you reach your full retirement age and are in that month then you can work and earn as much as you want and they won't decrement your retirement. In other words, someone born in December would be affected by the limit of $3740 per month more than the person born in February, because the person born in February, in that month of their full retirement age, can earn whatever they want and not be affected by the income limits. The other person has to wait until the following year to enjoy such a benefit. One last thing to address is that the Social Security administration is still, sort of, looking out for you, because obviously you are going to be paying social security taxes on that money you are earning and it could change the amount of your benefit. If it does, then they will alert you that your monthly benefit could change. In most of the cases, I am hoping you will be in, your benefits will not go up, because you will be receiving the maximum benefit already, and so the amount you get will not change. If this is not the case, they will let you know that your benefits may have increased because of your most recent earnings. I am trying to get you to a point where you do not need to work, but if you choose to then just be aware it has some impact on your social security benefits. Back to our question of what you live on if you do decide to stop working.

What you will be forced to live on if you decide to stop working is the retirement investments you made without the government's help. Look at the amount of money you are receiving (monthly) in each case. About $2000 at 62 going up to about $3300 when you are 70. What if you want to stop working at age 62, but decide to split the difference and wait until 67 to receive your social security benefits? You will not get any social security benefits for 5 years and then you will get an amount that is known as your full retirement amount. Another cash flow will show you what happens to your overall financial positon:

| Years | Beginning balance | Ending Balance |
|---|---|---|
| 62 | $400,000.00 | $402,060.67 |
| 63 | $402,060.67 | $404,125.41 |
| 64 | $404,125.41 | $406,328.42 |
| 65 | $406,328.42 | $408,678.98 |
| 66 | $408,678.98 | $411,186.95 |
| 67 | $411,186.95 | $430,483.15 |
| 68 | $430,483.15 | $451,071.65 |
| 69 | $451,071.65 | $473,038.99 |
| 70 | $473,038.99 | $496,477.53 |
| 71 | $496,477.53 | $521,485.79 |
| 72 | $521,485.79 | $548,168.91 |
| 73 | $548,168.91 | $576,639.04 |
| 74 | $576,639.04 | $607,015.86 |
| 75 | $607,015.86 | $639,427.08 |
| 76 | $639,427.08 | $674,008.94 |
| 77 | $674,008.94 | $710,906.81 |
| 78 | $710,906.81 | $750,275.80 |
| 79 | $750,275.80 | $792,281.40 |
| 80 | $792,281.40 | $837,100.20 |
| 81 | $837,100.20 | $884,920.59 |
| 82 | $884,920.59 | $935,943.61 |
| 83 | $935,943.61 | $990,383.73 |
| 84 | $990,383.73 | $1,048,469.80 |
| 85 | $1,048,469.80 | $1,110,446.01 |
| 86 | $1,110,446.01 | $1,176,572.88 |
| 87 | $1,176,572.88 | $1,247,128.39 |

The assumptions made in this table were an average annual return rate of 6.5%, and that you had a nest egg of $400,000, and that you only needed whatever social security was going to pay you at your full retirement age to live. Using those same assumptions though what happens if you were to still retire at 62, but start taking your retirement benefits right away:

| Years | Beginning balance | Ending Balance |
|---|---|---|
| 62 | $400,000.00 | $418,541.93 |
| 63 | $418,541.93 | $438,280.98 |
| 64 | $438,280.98 | $459,341.98 |
| 65 | $459,341.98 | $481,813.49 |
| 66 | $481,813.49 | $505,789.95 |
| 67 | $505,789.95 | $531,372.16 |
| 68 | $531,372.16 | $558,667.65 |
| 69 | $558,667.65 | $587,791.18 |
| 70 | $587,791.18 | $618,865.16 |
| 71 | $618,865.16 | $652,020.23 |
| 72 | $652,020.23 | $687,395.75 |
| 73 | $687,395.75 | $725,140.43 |
| 74 | $725,140.43 | $765,412.95 |
| 75 | $765,412.95 | $808,382.59 |
| 76 | $808,382.59 | $854,229.99 |
| 77 | $854,229.99 | $903,147.87 |
| 78 | $903,147.87 | $955,341.88 |
| 79 | $955,341.88 | $1,011,031.41 |
| 80 | $1,011,031.41 | $1,070,450.58 |
| 81 | $1,070,450.58 | $1,133,849.15 |
| 82 | $1,133,849.15 | $1,201,493.65 |
| 83 | $1,201,493.65 | $1,273,668.42 |
| 84 | $1,273,668.42 | $1,350,676.88 |
| 85 | $1,350,676.88 | $1,432,842.73 |
| 86 | $1,432,842.73 | $1,520,511.38 |
| 87 | $1,520,511.38 | $1,614,051.36 |

At 87 your retirement account would have about $366,923 more in it in the second scenario. Year 87 was chosen only to demonstrate 25 years of the bathtub retirement growth and withdrawal. I am not suggesting you will no longer be retired after 87 or deceased. If you live longer then you may want that retirement account to grow even further to support your continued need or to be passed down to whoever you so choose. Why you have more money in the second case, though, is because you are eating away less at your retirement account in those years you did not get any social security benefits in the first scenario. In the first scenario you must use more of the account, and every time you use the account to support yourself you are diminishing its growth. You are going to have to diminish the growth of the account to live, but we want to limit this erosion early on in order to preserve the account for longer. Those are the same years you want your retirement account to still fill with bathwater not remove more water. From a financial perspective I would suggest taking your benefits as soon as you can both to: secure what you get in case the government decides to change the rules again as well as to preserve your retirement account as much as you can. The government generally grandfathers you in on the old rules, if you are already receiving benefits, so, to me, money in my pocket now is worth more than waiting until later when I may, potentially, receive a little more money. If you are curious, the scenario only gets worse if you wait until 70, because then you are having to use more of your non-social security investments to live on while you do not receive these benefits. Why the government gives you these options to wait is also pretty clear when you view it from their financial perspective. The social security account is not unlike your retirement account. The government and you pay into this account with your taxes, and it grows over time, but as you take money out of it or more people draw on the account it can be like the bathtub with more money coming out than going in. This is the aggregate case of the account currently, and why you hear so much about the account running out of money. If more people wait then the account will be available for longer, because they make money on the money you do not draw for those years. Just like when you excitedly collect a tax refund each year thinking you are making money, but, in reality, you are losing money because the government was the one making money on the money they overdrew from your paychecks over the previous year. You also may not want to have any money in your personal retirement account when you die either, because ten you need to worry about estate planning and extra taxes. The way to do this is to tinker with the monthly installments you withdrawal from the account and watch the cash flow. If it goes negative before you project you will die then you are taking too much water from the bathtub, and you should take less. If it is still growing, you may want to think about taking more out.

## Financial Ninja

Once you have a smooth running retirement account you can begin to rest a little easier, because, as I described earlier, you can borrow from this retirement account to remedy some of the debt you accrue in the years preceding retirement. Let us hope you have planned well and do have money in a retirement account growing in, at least, a manner consistent with the scenarios described above, but what happens to all of the money you don't use? None of these cases, in my opinion, has the kind of overall growth I want to see in my retirement account in my retirement years. The reason is because what do you do with all of that money you did not use when you do die? Sure, you may have a spouse that is still living so you would want them to be able to live comfortably once you are gone, but it is still going to grow, and you may have been able to do something you did not get to do in your retirement years or you may be able to start your kids off on a better financial glideslope than the one you were on. You could give it to your children, but as a lump sum, they will be taxed on it more heavily than if it was not given to them in a lump. Ask anyone about the inheritance tax laws and you will quickly find out that they are not in favor of your money retaining its value. Once you get past your lifetime giving limit you start running into higher amounts being retained by the government as you transfer these funds. The lifetime giving limit is right around $2.5 million per person, and you may be saying to yourself you won't ever get to that limit, but look at the growth described in either scenario. Add to that any pension you may have or any other income stream and you can see if you live to a more seasoned year of, say, 90 you will start pushing those limits. You might not want to give it to your kids either, because perhaps you are estranged or for whatever reason, but either spend it or give some of it away earlier rather than waiting until you die. Few people understand the concept of transferring your wealth to other entities, but having a working knowledge of ways to properly transfer your wealth is certainly useful.

Let us assume you do want to transfer some of the surplus money from your retirement account, now that you have worked so hard to build it up, to your children. Let us further assume you have two children. Finally, let us also assume you had children when you were in your 30s so when you are in your 60s, in other words, when you are thinking about retiring or are retired, your kids will be in their 30s. Why not help them in these more formative years rather than waiting until you are 85 and your kids are 55 and nearing their own retirement. The good old IRS allows you to gift to your children, currently, $14,000 a year that they will not have to pay income tax on. The reason they won't have to pay income tax on it is because you already are paying income tax on it, so do not think the government is really giving you some sort of gift, because they are not. So let us relook at the same cash flow (we will use the wiser second scenario) and let us put some more realistic numbers in that cash flow. Let us assume that you were making $70,000 when you retired and you would like to maintain about 90% of that amount in your retirement years. That would be about $63,000. Social security, as I mentioned before, is not terribly easy to calculate, but if you were making $70,000 when you retired, we can assume you were making something less than that for the years they calculate what you will get back as a benefit finally culminating in your $70,000 current salary. Without needlessly complicating this scenario, let us assume, for social security purposes, your average earning salary was about $65,000, which should generate about $1650 a month, if you retire and take that money at 62. Let us also add in a little pension or something that gives you about $1000 dollars a month when you retire, and also, instead of $400,000, your retirement account grew to $500,000 before you started needing it. Finally, we won't add a spouse's numbers into this scenario, but, obviously, if you did the numbers would be greater, but so too would your need:

| Years | Beginning balance | Ending Balance |
|---|---|---|
| 62 | $500,000.00 | $501,339.44 |
| 63 | $501,339.44 | $502,594.45 |
| 64 | $502,594.45 | $503,933.52 |
| 65 | $503,933.52 | $505,362.26 |
| 66 | $505,362.26 | $506,886.69 |
| 67 | $506,886.69 | $508,513.22 |
| 68 | $508,513.22 | $510,248.67 |
| 69 | $510,248.67 | $512,100.36 |
| 70 | $512,100.36 | $514,076.05 |
| 71 | $514,076.05 | $516,184.06 |
| 72 | $516,184.06 | $518,433.25 |
| 73 | $518,433.25 | $520,833.07 |
| 74 | $520,833.07 | $523,393.61 |
| 75 | $523,393.61 | $526,125.63 |
| 76 | $526,125.63 | $529,040.62 |
| 77 | $529,040.62 | $532,150.83 |
| 78 | $532,150.83 | $535,469.35 |
| 79 | $535,469.35 | $539,010.10 |
| 80 | $539,010.10 | $542,787.99 |
| 81 | $542,787.99 | $546,818.89 |
| 82 | $546,818.89 | $551,119.75 |
| 83 | $551,119.75 | $555,708.65 |
| 84 | $555,708.65 | $560,604.87 |
| 85 | $560,604.87 | $565,829.00 |
| 86 | $565,829.00 | $571,403.00 |
| 87 | $571,403.00 | $577,350.30 |

In order to maintain an income of $63,000, you needed to withdrawal about another $2600 a month from your retirement account to make up the difference between the pension and your social security benefits, and that is what this cash flow shows. You are you are doing fine though, your money is still growing, albeit not nearly as much as the scenarios previously discussed. What you would not want to see is your money starting to decline significantly. If you did pass away at 87 in this scenario you would be leaving someone a little over half-a-million dollars. That is not over the lifetime limit so you will not be subject to the inheritance tax on top of all the other taxes, but it is still a lot to give at one time so perhaps we can do something to fix that. If you, instead, started transferring that wealth a little earlier instead of giving it all away at the end, what would happen. You could then find a number that would help your kids in those years when they could really use it to pay off their own debts, or save for a house, or pay childhood expenses of their own. If instead of taking out $2600 a month you took out $3000 a month that cash flow would look something more like this:

| Years | Beginning balance | Ending Balance |
| --- | --- | --- |
| 62 | $500,000.00 | $496,393.82 |
| 63 | $496,393.82 | $492,345.22 |
| 64 | $492,345.22 | $488,025.47 |
| 65 | $488,025.47 | $483,416.42 |
| 66 | $483,416.42 | $478,498.70 |
| 67 | $478,498.70 | $473,251.62 |
| 68 | $473,251.62 | $467,653.14 |
| 69 | $467,653.14 | $461,679.72 |
| 70 | $461,679.72 | $455,306.25 |
| 71 | $455,306.25 | $448,505.93 |
| 72 | $448,505.93 | $441,250.19 |
| 73 | $441,250.19 | $433,508.51 |
| 74 | $433,508.51 | $425,248.36 |
| 75 | $425,248.36 | $416,435.02 |
| 76 | $416,435.02 | $407,031.42 |
| 77 | $407,031.42 | $396,998.05 |
| 78 | $396,998.05 | $386,292.73 |
| 79 | $386,292.73 | $374,870.45 |
| 80 | $374,870.45 | $362,683.20 |
| 81 | $362,683.20 | $349,679.75 |
| 82 | $349,679.75 | $335,805.43 |
| 83 | $335,805.43 | $321,001.92 |
| 84 | $321,001.92 | $305,207.00 |
| 85 | $305,207.00 | $288,354.26 |
| 86 | $288,354.26 | $270,372.86 |
| 87 | $270,372.86 | $251,187.21 |

You are still not suffering since your income has not changed at all, but your kids are benefiting from the transfer of your wealth. Your money is now being transferred to your children at $200 a month for each child. That may not seem like a lot of money, but over a year it is $2400 each. That money could be then put into a college savings account for their children, or put into their own savings account, or used to start slashing into their own debts. It is not close to the limit of $14,000 each per year, but it is something that could make your children's lives better so that they don't find themselves having to fight debts their whole life as you have. If you carry out the cash flow even longer, you will see that at some point you will run out of money in that account, but hopefully that number is coincident with your passing. If you have done it right, all of your wealth is transferred to your children just as you pass away. This way they get the maximum benefit from that transferring of wealth in the years they can use it as opposed to waiting until you are 95 at which point they get $500,000 each and now have to figure out what they are going to do with that windfall. Since you are already paying taxes on that transfer the recipient will not be taxed on it as additional income, but another way of doing it is to open up a trust in their name and put money in that account which could help both of you. This helps you on your tax bill, because you will not be taxed on the money you put in the trust, but the recipient will. The idea is that they will probably be in a tax bracket that is less than one you are in so they will not pay as much tax on that money when they do finally take it out. Yet another way to transfer some of that wealth of yours could be to set up a 529 Education Plan with either the owner being the child parents or another person you specify via the Uniform Transfer to Minors Act (UTMA). The exact formula for what you should transfer earlier is, obviously, not possible but the point I am making, I think, is clear. If you have more money than you do not need for your own sustainment in your retirement portfolio then transfer it earlier rather than, as most people do, in a lump sum fashion. We have all heard stores of someone inheriting a large sum of money, and what I find bothersome about that is that they could have been better served having gotten that money over time instead of all at once. If you do not want to transfer your wealth to your children then give it to your cat, but again, I think the cat would rather have a bigger scratching post when he or she could use it rather than spend the extra money on a softer bed or a bigger scratching post when they can barely move.

    Let us examine further the amount you hope to live off of in your retirement, because this is one of those areas of financial planning that ultimately frustrated me, and partially why I decided to write this book. Most financial planners will ask you what you want to retire with, when I believe the question should be more on them to figure out how to maximize the amount of money you can have in your retirement years. As I said before, a benchmark often quoted is 80% of your before retirement income. They will tell you that you will have less bills and obligations in your retirement years so you do not need as much. I do not know if I would use that as a planning figure, though. I can assure you, you will also have some bills that you did not have, or are bigger than, when you were younger, and medical expenses are one of them. I don't want to begin to tell you how to navigate those waters, but suffice it to say that Medicare and Medicate is not as cheap as you might think. Also, the medical care you can actually get on those plans alone may seem like quality care when you are younger and, arguably, invincible, but it is not as glorious in execution. The standard monthly payment for Medicare is just about 100 dollars a month per person, so both you and your spouse will need to kick in $100. Also, if you make over $85,000, currently, you will need to pay nearly $30 more per month per person for coverage. If you need prescriptions, you will need get part D, which could add another 12 dollars a month to that amount. Then you will need to pay out of pocket for the care you do get on the first $165 you pay for medical care—again, for each person. Once you outlay $165 then your visits are covered entirely by Medicare, but that averages about $125 to $150 a month just in coverage costs—per person. This does not include all of the incidentals associated with longer term ailments or any other expenses you may have now that you are retired.

    You may also want to look into long term health care plans as well, and I can tell you for a fact these are not cheap either. The reason they are not cheap is because the company providing the coverage knows that medical expenses are high so in order to maintain a profit margin they have to pass these higher costs on to you. Frankly, I am not a big fan of long term health care plans, because if I have saved well enough for my retirement I should not need one. It is like insurance. You are paying for peace of mind, but the company providing the coverage charges you for that peace of mind. If I am at a point where I need such extensive care to maintain my very existence than just push me over a cliff and be done with me. I want to live it up while I am ambulatory. Long term health care plans can cost you upwards of $500 a month that you would need to start paying in your 40's to be able to take advantage of some 30 years later. I, personally, would rather take that $500 a month and invest it separately in an interest bearing account and use that money, if I need it, to offset any long term health care costs I may encounter later. If it turns out I don't need the long term care then all of that investment turns into boats and better vacations before I become confined to a bed.

Retirement planning is not difficult. It just takes some deliberate planning before you retire and stop working. Undoubtedly, you have heard the same figures I have for how little, on average, people are saving for their retirement. No financial planner will disagree that earlier is better than later, but taking advantage of the minimums available to you is all I am asking you to consider, because at least with a modest 401(k), or an IRA, and some sort of government benefit you should be better off than someone who decided to spend all of their money and hope that government programs will be sufficient to sustain them in their golden years.

# CHAPTER 5—BUDGETING AND SAVING

*It is not common knowledge that being poor can also hamper your ability to interact socially, which can have lasting effects. You don't have the opportunity to interact with people from stations that are much outside your own. When I was growing up, if we were fortunate enough to meet someone with whom we would like to have interacted, our house didn't lend itself very well to entertaining these potential guests. First my parents, or at least my mother, collected pets, and gave decisions usually reserved for adults to her children. Like the time she asked if my oldest brother would like a dog. He, of course, gave a resounding affirmation, but then when it came time to choose the pet somehow he decided a Great Pyrenees was the dog he should have. Just born these dogs are big. At adulthood, the dog weighted over 110 pounds. In a house of only 750 square feet of living space, this was like having another full grown human in the house. The dog was also accustom to a more rugged environment as well, and quickly ate a hole in the carpet as well as my brothers foam mattress. My father repaired both of these in the most industrial manner possible including: highly visible tacks in the floor and simply making my brother have to pile the clumps of foam back in his bed at each sheet changing to make something like a mattress. My father also had 2 snakes in aquariums in our tiny little living room. These tanks were placed on top of weak plywood console, which bowed under the pressure of the tanks as well as all the complementary florescent lighting; not exactly the welcoming environment someone hopes to find when entering someone's home. Clumping and odor controlling kitty litter did not exist either so there was a constant miasma of cat pee and two-packs-a-day worth of cigarette smoke swirling in the air. I only recently realized all interior paint was not dingy yellow in color. The daily delivery of newspapers contributed to cramped living spaces as these were shoved under anything which had legs even though we would routinely bag them up and send them to recycling facilities. Having but one bathroom also would lead to some eventful nights should someone sleep-over and find themselves having to pee in the middle of the night amid the frightening sight of my mother sitting on the one toilet blinking in the now flood of light they provided to navigate their own way in the bathroom. Upon their return, since space was limited, they would return to the room only to find their sleeping bag melted and was now sticking to the dangerous low-income housing baseboard heating units. While we had grown accustom to such an environment, I can only imagine the stories these kids told their parents upon their return. There were seldom repeat guests so I intuit they were forbade from returning. Needless to say, I didn't have many friends as a child and didn't really understand how to cultivate these kinds of relationships through lack of experience.*

    Budgeting is another area upon which people will give you circumspect advice. Everyone understands the basic idea of a budget and savings, but no one really explains a solid plan to manage your income and the outflow of expenses. I am hoping to lift that veil, and give you some simple tools to make a rudimentary, but powerful, budget that takes into account your general financial situation, your current financial situation, and allows for future planning. How do you build this simple budget tool, well, with a modicum of understanding you can build one in Excel that I content will rival most other commercially offered tools. The first part is your general financial situation:

| | |
|---|---:|
| Cell phone | 166 |
| Cable | 70 |
| Car Insurance | 95 |
| Life Insurance | 23 |
| Food | 800 |
| Home Owners | 65 |
| College saving | 100 |
| Mortgage/Rent | 1500 |
| Elec | 175 |
| Daycare | 100 |
| Dining Out | 62 |
| Credit Card 1 | 300 |
| Water/garbage | 145 |
| Credit Card 2 | 60 |
| Amazon | 75 |
| Gas | 110 |
| Car loan | 567 |
| Credit Card 3 | 300 |
| Total | 4713 |
| | |
| Monthly Pay | 5000 |
| | |
| Leftover | 287 |

# Financial Ninja

Something like this shows how healthy you are monthly, and about what you should have left over each month. I have spread out bills like car insurance into a monthly bill, because often times this bill comes only once every six months but you should budget for it on a monthly basis. That is why I allotted, in this case, 95 dollars a month so that when the six month premium becomes due for $570 I am prepared. This could apply to other bills as well that come with a periodicity other than monthly. Also, because the table of numbers are made off of averages you need to have a second part of this budget tool that shows you what is occurring from paycheck to paycheck, because that is how you really operate:

|        | Column A | Column B | Column C         | Column D | Column E |
|--------|----------|----------|------------------|----------|----------|
| 21-Apr | 2307     | 400      | Food             |          |          |
|        |          | 75       | Amazon Card      |          |          |
|        |          | 68       | Cable            |          |          |
|        |          | 100      | College Savings  |          |          |
|        |          | 195      | Home Owners Ins. |          |          |
|        |          | 24       | Amazon purchase  |          |          |
|        |          |          |                  | save     | 1200     |
|        |          |          |                  | 1445     |          |
|        |          |          |                  | 245      |          |
| 5-May  | 2307     | 1500     | Mortgage         |          |          |
|        | 1200     | 10       | Magazine Sub.    |          |          |
|        |          | 75       | Credit card 1    |          |          |
|        |          | 300      | Credit Card 2    |          |          |
|        |          | 300      | Water/Garbage    |          |          |
|        |          | 176      | Power            |          |          |
|        |          | 400      | Food             |          |          |
|        |          | 567      | Car              |          |          |
|        |          |          |                  | 179      |          |

This part of the budget is real-time so it shows what you actually have left from paycheck to paycheck. Two things may make it different than what you calculate in the aggregated budget. One is that you probably get paid on a biweekly basis, that would give you 26 paychecks over a year, which is not quite twice a month. Your monthly budget is, therefore, probably not aligned with the real-time budget. The second things that could make them different is because you will record more in the paycheck look budget than you will the overall monthly budget. You can feel those things that are closer to you like an unforeseen car repair or a wardrobe upgrade due to a really good sale.

Column A contains what you expect to get in from each paycheck. Notice there is an extra 1200 dollars listed on May $5^{th}$. This is because your bills don't really care when you get paid, so in order for your budget to meet all the needs of your bill due dates you have to sometimes save, or hold back, money from a previous paycheck in order to make a necessary bigger bills in a future period. This is the "budgeting" part of a budget. It will ensure you are, at least, aware of your financial situation at the time you get each paycheck. I know it isn't comfortable living paycheck to paycheck, but living paycheck to paycheck is better than not having enough at a particular paycheck and having to not pay something or pay it late with the requisite late fees. More on late fees later. Column B are those bills, or expenditures, you expect to have to make from one pay period to the next, with the current paycheck. Be sure to include everything here. This is where you would include the unforeseen car repair or the new shoes you want to buy or bought. You may have more than what is in part one of the budget where you outline your general health. You will know if you can afford those items in that pay period or not if you record more than just the general monthly bills. Column C is just a description of what the expenditure is so that you know what it is you are paying or budgeting for. You can put anything you want in here, and also color coding thing is another method to ensure you capture things that you might otherwise miss. Some bills are only due on a quarterly basis, so indicating that you paid that bill in a particular period can help you when, or if, you need to go back and reconcile your expenses. Column D is a simple formula calculation which takes the sum of Column A (all income for the period including anything you withheld from a previous period) for the period and subtracts out the sum of

Column B (expenses) for the period. In our example, for May 5th that math would be:(2307 + 1200) − (1500 + 10 + 75 + 300 + 300 + 176 + 400 + 567) = 179. The last column is to capture any savings you may need to do during a period to either meet the next period's bills or it may be a place to put savings you are developing to buy something outside your normal budget, like Christmas gifts, or saving for a vacation. I know this all sounds very simple and there are plenty of programs on the market that do much of this for you, but buying an additional budget tracker, to me, is like buying an egg slicer. It works fine for that one task, but unless I am eating sliced eggs nearly every day, I hardly think the use justifies the cost. *Excel* or other spreadsheet programs are not egg slicers. They have buried in them, lots of capability you can use, but for budgeting you don't need much more than I am outlining here. When you in fact pay the bill is also important to record so I would highlight the cell when you pay the actual bill. That way you can reconcile what appears here with what any of your bank's financial records should show. This can be used to plan for several months of paychecks including perturbations that may occur later in the year, like having to pay for summer camps for your kids or any expense that is not typically listed on your part one overall budget. Once you have executed all of the expenses for one paycheck, I recommend keeping, at least, the one previous period. You can delete those rows associated with a period before the previous period, move the future paycheck period up and add another one in the future. This revolving real-time budget gives you a solid view of what you have moment to moment. I recommend a less revolving one, and instead recommend keeping about 3 months of both previous and future periods. I recommend doing this because if you have some catching up to do, or you are paying down credit cards, or you are saving for something, so that you can view previous activities. When you are finally comfortable with how you have executed a period of time, be it shorter periods or a three to six month period, then you can delete that section. The less certain your financial situation the longer period of time I would keep. I wouldn't keep more than a year, because otherwise you are going to get lost again and it won't really provide you any really useful information, and may be the reason you are in the financial situation you are in now.

Part three of the overall budget is where you can project raises and various other bigger changes in your financial situation. It is also how you can project what your game plan for paying down your debt in the future will look like. The format is similar to the part one shown earlier, but it would include those things that you project to change in the future:

| | |
|---|---|
| Cell phone | 166 |
| Cable | 70 |
| Car Insurance | 95 |
| Life Insurance | 23 |
| Food | 800 |
| Home Owners | 65 |
| College saving | 100 |
| Mortgage/Rent | 1500 |
| Elec | 175 |
| Daycare | 100 |
| Dining Out | 62 |
| Credit Card 1 | |
| Water/garbage | 145 |
| Credit Card 2 | 360 |
| Amazon | 75 |
| Gas | 110 |
| Car loan | 567 |
| Credit Card 3 | 300 |
| Total | 4713 |
| | |
| Monthly Pay | 5000 |
| | |
| Leftover | 287 |

Notice here I have managed to pay off credit card 1 so that block goes away, and I can now put toward Credit card 2 the $300 I was putting toward Credit Card 1 or I can put that money toward something else, but knowing what you are going to do with any changes in your income or expenses in the future now gives you a complete picture of your finances. This also allows for you to project savings in the future.

We have looked at one form of savings which was your retirement account, but trying to build up a robust savings of cash on hand can be useful as well. Most planners will recommend you have 2 months of your salary in savings so that you can weather some financial storms that may hit, like being laid off for a period of time, or if you should switch jobs. I don't disagree with this in theory, but it is a lot harder to do in practice. Paying down your credit card debts is better than saving money for a rainy day. Your credit card debt is providing you plenty of rain already so get rid of that first before you build up a savings. Also, if you are having trouble building up a savings don't dismiss the paid off credit card and how it can be used to provide you some security against life changes. That is a veiled security blanket, because you can use it to pay for unforeseen car repairs and then start right away on the techniques above, and outlined in other chapters, to bring that card back down to a zero balance so that it is available for the next unforeseen expense. If your furnace breaks and you need a new one, but having not saved two months' worth of your salary you can use that credit card to buy the new furnace or repair the old one, and then just use the methods we have learned to pay that card down again with the hope of not needing it in the future. What I certainly would not do is have a robust savings along with significant balances on your credit cards. It defeats the savings, because you are losing money while you are making hardly any money in savings interest on the money you are retaining for a rainy day. Instead, pay down those cards, use the free balances as your emergency fund, and then try to build up a savings to use instead of credit at a point when you are more financially solvent. Making 1.5% on a savings account while you are paying 10%, or more, on a credit card balance is a net loss of, at least, 8.5% or more. That doesn't make financial sense, and our goal is to live sensibly.

## Jason Evans

One unforeseen expense that can really hurt both your budget and your credit is a medical expense. So let us discuss this specific expense. The reason it can hurt both is because hospitals and clinics don't have the ability to manage payments like a fully staffed bank so when you decide, or forget, to pay one of these out of cycle or unexpected bills the clinic or hospital will likely send that bill right away to a collection entity, which has one goal in mind—making your life financially painful until you pay off the outstanding debt. Coincident with all the calls the collection agency will engage in is that they will greatly harm your credit, or at least try to, and you want to avoid marring your credit, particularly because this may be a small bill that you could have paid off had you been more vigilant when it came separately in the mailbox you seldom check anymore.

Once a collection or late payment gets on your credit record it is very difficult to get it removed. That is why we want to try to avoid it getting on there in the first place. It is difficult to remove for several reasons. The credit agency in its pursuit to satisfy its banking customers wants to ensure that negative information is quickly accessible so that the bank can have a complete, although often flawed, view of your financial aptitude. Also, the way they collect information and update their records tends to lean toward keeping information on the report rather than removing it. Even though they tell you things like a bankruptcy or foreclosure will stay on there for only seven to ten years anyone who has just waited them out and expected it to be removed is quickly disabused of that notion when, after all of that waiting, low and behold it is still there seven years later. Significantly negative information is removable in that timeframe if you satisfy the debt or if you have court documents that specify how the debts will be reflected on your credit report. That timeframe also assumes you have been vigilantly monitoring the information as well. Removing the information requires someone to go in and change your file, which is additional work that doesn't create profit for the reporting agency so there is little motivation on their part to remove it. In other words, the only one who is really working for your credit report is you, so do your best to protect it.

If you do dispute the credit rating or information you are in for a fight. There have been some improvements in this process, but it is still largely impersonal and, ultimately, if the credit reporting agency wants to keep something on there you will drain your retirement account in legal fees before it is removed. This is why I suggest you try not to get negative information on there in the first place.

There is an important note about disputing that you can use to your advantage, though. This wasn't always the case, but credit reporting legislation has put some binding on the credit agency's seemingly unchecked power. If you dispute something now, for the period of time when the item is in dispute they have to calculate, but may not always do this so make sure they do, your score without taking that negative information into account. How you can use it to your advantage is when you are disputing something your credit score could go up allowing you to get better rates and terms to be able to do the things I outline in other chapters. When you apply for a credit card the results come back quickly because it is all done electronically, and unless the reader of that inquiry is diligent they may not see that you are disputing something so your score is artificially (not artificially if you do win your dispute) inflated. I will caution you though that this won't work for things like a home purchase, because now banks scrutinize your credit quite a bit more than they did before the housing market collapsed. If you are applying for a home they may even tell you to remove your dispute or risk not getting a loan until the dispute is fully satisfied so that they can see where your real score lies. Again, this is not a method I would use on a regular basis either, but used wisely to get yourself in a position to then pay off your debt with better terms is only using legal tools available to you to your advantage.

Jason Evans

The credit reporting agencies are not on your side. They don't fight you fairly so you don't have to fight them fairly.

Another way they are not on your side is by offering you credit monitoring. Although they certainly make it seem like this is the panacea to all of your financial problems, it is not. This is just another way for them to extricate you of your hard earned dollars. As I mentioned before, most banks, and even quite a few credit cards, now offer some level of credit monitoring or your FICO score for free, so paying a credit agency to do it for you each month is absolutely absurd. They will try to sell you on the idea that you get constant credit monitoring, but who needs such monitoring? For most of us our credit score, and history, is not going to change on a monthly basis so all those months that you paid for the service and received a report that was identical to the previous month you wasted your money. Often, the information that is on these reports lags anyway so any monitoring won't change the amount of time it takes for information to be updated. You are not in the special "no wait" line at a water park. You are just paying them for a service that is already largely offered to you for free by other institutions with whom you already engage. They will also claim that this monitoring will protect you from fraud or, at least, alert you to such fraudulent activity, but again, unless I have millions of dollars that I am protecting, what they are protecting is worth less than the cost to protect it. Banks will generally tell you when your card or cards are being used inappropriately and will stop payment fairly quickly. Banks are even required to keep on hand money to satisfy bad accounts or cover fraudulent activities so you won't be responsible for the charges fraudulently put on your account. As long as you didn't get so fooled that you actually authorized the credit transaction the bank will usually put the money back into your account, and even FEDEX you a new card the next day, if you are at a location other than your home, and this is often free as well. I have been a first-hand recipient of the banks monitoring ability a few times. I have been on vacation and forgot to indicate that to the bank holding my credit card as I went to the grocery store to purchase some incidentals and my card was denied, because the bank assume my purchase across the country was not legitimate. I would rather have them err or the side of caution then let such purchase go, perhaps I am in a minority here, but paying for additional monitoring is, to me, ludicrous.

Armed with a budget as we have developed here, and an understanding of how to pay your bills as well as monitoring your own credit you can, and will, ensure you take care of your current obligations and can project into the future. I have outlined a plan that is not so onerous that you don't want to do it either. If you were to look at this for 10 minutes a week, you could very easily keep your finances in order and not become overwhelmed by your financial health or future. It is also something you can develop without having to spend additional money for an expensive budgeting tool that will have a much prettier layout, but won't provide you any more utility than what I have given you here.

## CHAPTER 6—COLLEGE SAVINGS

*My parents didn't go to college when they were younger, and my father never went to college. Therefore, when it came time for us to go to college or not go to college, as my father suggested, we were ill-prepared. I didn't know how to go about applying, and what tests were necessary to get the chance to be accepted. I also didn't know what it would cost. When I did get accepted I didn't know what to do when I got there or how to manage the workload. Despite what they say high school does not prepare you for the biggest problem that will face children when they go to college—supervision.*

## Financial Ninja

*I had come from a poor background and because of that I managed to secure some scholarship money. I was, essentially, given money each quarter and then left to decide both: what to do with that money and how to manage my own workload. I knew the only thing I needed to do was maintain a particular grade point average to keep the flow of quarterly money going. I didn't have a budget, and I didn't have a clear understanding of credit. I used the money I got in month one of the new quarter and then when month two rolled around I was eating ramen noodles, with the very highly MSG laced packets, for most of the rest of that quarter until a new invagination of money magically appeared in my account. I still thank the lack of technology which allowed me to float checks for three or more days; something today's youth have no idea about. With instant transactions I would have been eating the package the ramen came in for at least two days as I waited for new money.*

*Managing my time wasn't much easier. Picking your own classes was done over the phone and so in order to get the good classes you had to both: get up early and be pretty quick with the dialer as you retyped the number to keep trying to break into an opportunity to pick classes you needed. At the time, I felt sleep was way more important so I was left to choose classes that were not at the most optimal times, or classes I didn't even want, to maintain a full-time class load. Without supervision I was also less than exemplary on my attendance record. All though elementary school and high school I prided myself on this fairly easy milestone to cross, but once I got to college it seemed an impossible task. I had to decide between getting up and going to a class or going to the very well stocked intermural gym. I often chose the gym because it didn't have attendance grades or very many tests save the occasional, friendly, bench-press challenge.*

*Ultimately, I did find my footing right about the third year of college, and managed to graduate, but having had some supervision before going would have made my time in college much more productive.*

## Jason Evans

Saving for your children's future education costs can be one of the biggest expenditures you will make, and also cause for one of the biggest headaches you are likely to have. While higher education has largely become a business of its own, with ever increasing tuition that may one day even outpace the benefits, it is still, often, an entrance fee to jobs that pay more, on average, than jobs that do not have higher education requirements. So how can this headache become more of a temporary migraine is just like everything else we have considered. The key is being aware of the things available to you as well as careful planning. What I want to ensure is that you are planning so that your plan is adaptable, solvent, and does not hurt your overall financial plans.

Again, the earlier you start the better, but if you didn't plan right away there are still plenty of ways to mitigate this expense. If you open up a savings account for each of your children, with even a modest investment, as soon as they are born it is very likely you would have enough to cover most university expenses. I say most, because out-of-state tuition and private, or Ivy league schools, could easily consume your investments at a rate much faster than the preceding years of returns. This is a simple future value cash flow if you were to invest 200 dollars a month for 18 years:

# Financial Ninja

| Monthly Investment | Year | What it will grow to at 6% |
|---|---|---|
| $200.00 | 1 | $2,467.11 |
| $200.00 | 2 | $5,086.39 |
| $200.00 | 3 | $7,867.22 |
| $200.00 | 4 | $10,819.57 |
| $200.00 | 5 | $13,954.01 |
| $200.00 | 6 | $17,281.77 |
| $200.00 | 7 | $20,814.79 |
| $200.00 | 8 | $24,565.71 |
| $200.00 | 9 | $28,547.98 |
| $200.00 | 10 | $32,775.87 |
| $200.00 | 11 | $37,264.53 |
| $200.00 | 12 | $42,030.03 |
| $200.00 | 13 | $47,089.47 |
| $200.00 | 14 | $52,460.95 |
| $200.00 | 15 | $58,163.74 |
| $200.00 | 16 | $64,218.27 |
| $200.00 | 17 | $70,646.22 |
| $200.00 | 18 | $77,470.64 |

    One thing to consider is when your child will actually start school. Most people assume right after high school is the best time to go to college, but I don't necessarily agree with this idea. College is (likely) a period of time when your child will be expected to be more independent than they heretofore have experienced. If they don't attend a school locally, and are not living at home to go to school, they will be confronted with both school and living challenges that you have insulated them from. What if they wait a year or two between high school and starting college? I can tell you two things that are likely to occur. One, that child will, more often than not, be more responsible. You could even use those two years to help them become more independent, and responsible, by allowing them to live on their own away from home. They could even take on enrichment opportunities that will make them a better applicant when they do apply to school. Extracurricular activities are often times of greater value than a high Grade Point Average (GPA). The other thing that will happen is your our investments are likely to grow by quite a bit in those extra two years. Look at what happens to that same cash flow adding just two more years:

| Monthly Investment | Year | What it will grow to at 6% |
|---|---|---|
| $200.00 | 19 | $84,715.97 |
| $200.00 | 20 | $92,408.18 |

Just in those last two extra years your investment in their education went from $77,470.64 to $92,408.18. That is an additional $14,937.54. In today's dollars, that is almost another year of tuition. So what would it be if you decided to not invest in the account the monthly contributions you had been making, but still wait the two years to have them start using the account for school expenses?

| Monthly Investment | Year | What it will grow to at 6% |
|---|---|---|
|  | 19 | $82,248.86 |
|  | 20 | $87,321.79 |

It still goes up $9,851.15. That is still a lot more money than what they would have had available after 18 years, and don't forget two more years of maturity, hopefully, in your child. The next thing to consider is where you should put your money to have it available for their schooling.

Typically, the route chosen for most of us to save for our children's college expenses is a 529. Most states offer some form of these, and some states even give you a tax break on the contributions, but generally these contributions do not receive a tax break. The contribution are tax free on the tail end when you withdrawal them for higher education expenses, but only for higher education expenses. Expenses can come in the form of: tuition, books, fees to go to the school, and even room and board. What people don't necessarily know is that these funds can also be used for expenses other than your typical two or four year college. They can be used to fund: culinary school, or flight school, or other trade school educations. Look closely at what the rules are with regard to the 529 you invest in. This give them higher marks in my opinion, because they are somewhat flexible, however, they must be used on education, which is a drawback if your child decides not to use them for higher education. You are going to take a 10% penalty to remove the funds on top of the now higher income you will have and the corresponding higher income taxes you will pay on that money once you have to withdrawal it.

You could, of course, take the same $50,000 loan we spoke about before and that would give you $50,000 that you would be paying back to yourself for their education over the next five years. This is recommended over taking the money directly from your retirement account, provided you are still about five years away from retiring.

People talk about penalty free withdrawals from you retirement account for education expenses, but what they may not tell you is that you will still, very likely, be subject to the 10% penalty even though they let you withdrawal it. It wouldn't be my first place to go to pay for my child's education. You can take out money under hardship conditions for several classes of expenses, but a first time home purchase and higher education are still subject to the penalty, so they are not truly penalty free. Better would be to borrow from your retirement account and pay yourself back. Roth IRAs are slightly different in that you can take your contributions back, but these will still add to your personal income and therefore now be taxed, probably, at a higher rate since you will be taking a significant amount out. Also, there are some important rules that could affect their eligibility for financial aid in the next year.

Financial aid is something few parents really understand. Your child's eligibility is affected by your income and assets, because the thinking is that if you have more you should spend it on your child's education so that the limited government funds can then be used on more needy children.

Jason Evans

Generally, though, student loans are available to most college bound students yet I see countless people not taking advantage of this opportunity. They see loan and they shy away, but it isn't like a credit card debt. It, generally, comes with a lower interest rate, and some of it is deferred (meaning you won't accrue interest until you, or they, finish school). When you fill out your financial aid forms these loan amounts take into consideration your living expenses as well, and since you will need to live somewhere don't just take what will cover your school expenses. Well, don't just take enough to cover school expenses unless you have a place to live already, like your parent's house or someone else who is covering your living expenses. If that is not the case, then take as much as they will give you. The point of school is to get you a job that pays more than you would be able to get without such an education. That education comes at a price, but as long as the price is less than what you could earn in the years following college then you should take the money. Even if it does not garner you a greater salary, you may want to take it because you may need the education to be in a job that you love, but just does not pay as much as other jobs. Perhaps, you are more interested in job satisfaction than more money from the actual job. Some loans backed by the government can also be forgiven if you satisfy certain conditions after you finish school. One thing I would definitely not recommend is not paying back these loans. They won't start becoming due until six months after you graduate, but defaulting on these loans will haunt you much more than would defaulting on a consumer loan. At some point there may be action taken by the institution who granted you the loan to garnish your wages, which is something a consumer loan cannot generally do.

Student loans are one of the few loans you can get that isn't backed by anything and the interest rates are generally lower than traditional credit loans, and with deferment or loan forgiveness, these loans become even more valuable. Or put another way, that student loan causes you less wealth erosion than it would to get the same amount of money some other way. Interest rates on student loans are set by Congress, and they vary depending on the type of loan you get, and for what the loan is used. They can be either: subsidized or unsubsidized. If you are getting your first undergraduate degree, depending on your need, your loan will likely be subsidized. This means the government, more specifically, the Department of Education, pays the interest on these direct subsidized loans while you are in school taking, at least, a "half-time" class load. They also cover that interest for the first six months after you finish school so these are the best kinds of loans. Deferment of the loan while you are in school is a big deal. You have seen in many of the other cash flows I showed you where just one year of interest can add up, so to have the original loan balance be the thing you start with six months *after* you finish school can really save you money. The rates are also pretty reasonable, considering you are not backing this loan with any collateral. For the 2017 school year, these rates varied from as low as 3.4% up to almost 7%. If you or your child is using the money for graduate school then the rates tend to be a little higher, and there is a good chance the loan will be unsubsidized, but these rates are much lower than most credit cards. Unsubsidized means the interest will start accruing right away, and I realize that sounds painful, but the rates are still less than what most credit cards offer. If you were to get a loan, other than from your retirement account, you would likely need to back it with some form of collateral or the rates could be much higher. The good thing about an unsubsidized student loan is that you don't have to demonstrate financial need to get one. The school won't give enough money to buy a boat and retire so that you can run away and default on it, but they will give you some. You can defer your payments, meaning you won't have to pay during the time you are going to school, but just realize interest will continue to add to the balance you will owe once you are done. The grace period is in name only, because you are still accruing interest in that period also. Something you can do though is to have your child take out the loan and you do your best to cover the payments while they are in school or part of the payments, because, again, you are getting a loan at a better rate than you would if you were to use your credit card to pay for their school or take a loan out directly from a bank and then use that money to pay for their school.

Being a dependent or independent student has some baring on how much they will be able to borrow, and for how much they are eligible, in total, for financial aid. Being a dependent is generally what a child is until they turn 24 years old or have emancipated themselves from you as their parents. The problem with them being a dependent, and you not being able to afford their college, is that your income still counts against them for the purposes of financial need. The government expects you to pay for your child's education with some of your income so do keep that in mind when you have children, but do not do anything to save for their continued education. The worst situation for a prospective college bound student is for the parents to have money, but not share that money with their children. I don't want you to do that or feel you have to do that, since there are ways to still help your child go to school even if you didn't have the foresight to have saved earlier for them. If your child is over 24 or meets some other qualifications like: being married or a member of the armed forces, they are considered independent and so do not have to share their parent's income information as part of their financial disclosure.

An ancillary benefit to your child is paying their loans with your money, if you can afford it. They still build a credit history, which, as I have mentioned in other chapters, is important so that they can begin to be in a position, hopefully, like you are with good credit and a decent income. If you can't help them pay the loans it is still, in my opinion, a very good idea for them to take out loans to pay for school and living expenses they will need to cover while they are in school. Obviously, you want to maximize any grants or other forms of money to use for college expenses, but right after that you want to maximize your student loan, or the student loan of your child going to school. One thing you can do for your children if you were not able to save before they went to school is to help them after they finish school. If you took on the payments for your child's student loan it is still you paying for their schooling. There is no shame in doing it after the fact. The goal is to help them get the degree. It shouldn't matter if you had the means available to save when they were younger or you adopt their student loans for them. If you can't adopt the whole student loan for them, you can still help them with the payments until they find the means to cover the payments for themselves.

## CHAPTER 7—FINAL THOUGHTS

    Most people don't grow up thinking they want to be poor, not care about credit, or do not want to own either a car or a home. Not having money is an insidious, cancer like, development. If your parents were poor, like mine, then it is hard to learn the skills necessary to manage money. It also makes it harder to set your children up on the path to financial security since you yourself must struggle to make ends meet. Not only because you don't have the means to do so, but you haven't mastered the financial landscape either, so helping someone else manage it is just that much more difficult. Being poor, and not having the skills required to become financially independent can span generations, and often does. It isn't just lack of money that keeps people poor, it is lack of skills as well. One can't expect to be a concert pianist without, at least, a modicum of practice, and financial management is not different. It just isn't very interesting to most people. There are certainly more lively pursuits, but, unfortunately, unless you, at a minimum, perform at the junior varsity level with regard to your finances you, and possibly your progeny, will not have the opportunity to pursue the more interesting things they really want to do. Therefore, I believe it behooves you to have a working knowledge of finances. My approach is to provide you not only a working knowledge, but the ability to transcend the varsity level, and become a financial ninja. Understanding how financial institutions work is the key to ensuring you can stay ahead. I do not mean you need to be able to take advantage of them, or do anything nefarious, but simply to navigate in waters for which they determine the current. What keeps people from understanding these waters is lack of good information. We all get plenty of digital, and printed, media messages suggesting ways to get out of financial burdens. It is determining which of these are legitimate and which are simply palliatives that will further trap you in the confines of debt that is the real art. We have all heard how devastating cash lending or payday loans can be, but when we find ourselves deciding between our toddler having something to eat and a 23% interest rate on that short term loan we would clearly choose our child eating. It doesn't have to come to making such decisions though. I am also not going to fault anyone who is forced to make such a decision. I want to help you build a financial future that ensures you will not have to make such decisions, though. I promise, if you work hard at applying the techniques I have outlined here in this book, your situation will go from dire to something more manageable to something fruitful. The thing that is keeping us poor is our fear, but don't let that fear make you a slave to debt or someone who must live on means that do not afford you the things you want and need.

## Jason Evans

What about having a money manager do all of this for me? While I don't disagree with the use of financial or wealth management, the issue I do have is most of the stuff they are going to do for you are things you can do for yourself. They are just going to charge you a fee to do it. One that, like interest on a loan, is going to erode your wealth. It may not be much, and they will contend the money you are paying them is going to be far less than what they are making you in the form of wealth building, but it is still erosion. That too may be true, and not unlike car repairs, it may make more sense for someone to fix your car rather than you learning how to fix it yourself with *YouTube* videos. The issue I have with financial managers is they don't necessarily have your best interest in mind. They are paid off actions taken on your behalf. Because of this, they have an incentive to take action, not sit idly by while the market itself makes your money grow. They may not think it is advisable to pay off debt when you could be investing it at a commission to them. If that debt is at the typical rates you are seeing on your credit cards then they are absolutely wrong to have you invest in something else in lieu of paying off that credit card debt. If that card is at 14%, and the financial manager is making you a good rate of return at 10%, annually, yet taking 1.5% in commission to do so, you are making an, effective, rate of only 8.5% on that investment while you are paying 14% to carry the debt. It would make more sense to not make that investment until you have paid off that debt, but the financial manager doesn't make any money when you do that.

You have to be ever vigilant when it comes to your money. A financial manager is great, if you already have a lot of money, and that is the goal I have for you. I want you to be, at least, as aware of how to change the oil filter on your car as you are about your finances so that you can save on routine financial maintenance until you get to the point where it is actually becoming cumbersome for you to manage it yourself. That is very different than giving away management before it is cumbersome. You should now have tools that are not only nearly as effective as those a financial manager has, but, are rather, equally as effective. You also know your situation better than they do.

## Financial Ninja

Your situation is unique, and while they can ask you all the right questions and get to what are your general goals, they cannot fully understand your risk posture or understand what your emotional attachment to your finances may be. Yes, I say emotional, because like the emotional attachment you may have had to your first car, people have emotional attachments to debts or to the lack of funds you have to fulfill your physical needs. If people were not so emotionally attached to their finances then we would have far fewer people seeking stress counseling.

I would like to get you to a state of understanding your finances that, if you are looking to have someone else manage your wealth for you, you understand what questions to ask them, not the other way around. If they are suggesting you buy life insurance, why are they suggesting whole as opposed to term. Is it because it makes financial sense to you, and your situation, or does it make sense *and* they make a little more commission, if they sell you that package. I am not suggesting that these financial managers are doing anything to outright mislead you, but they have children and families to feed as well. If they don't meet their work goals, they may be in a worse financial situation than you currently find yourself. My point is, be wary of anything anyone wants to do with your money. Are you getting what you are paying for? We have all read countless stories of people who win it big, only to lose that money shortly after they won it. They may have suddenly come into a lot more money than you currently have, but they were never taught the basics of money management, or how financial instruments are related, or how some places to put your winners are better than others. Do not let that happen to you.

There are also many more complicated topics I did not address. Investing itself is a complicated process. There are futures, options, and commodity trades that can build your wealth or help hedge against other market investments you may have. You can learn about these topics once you get yourself financially healthy. I am not trying to make you anything more than a ninja willing to use unconventional methods to achieving financial stability, and success, for what is your very unique situation.

Exercise the financial understanding I have tried to impart to you. If you don't agree with something I am espousing in this book than by all means learn for yourself what you believe is the right path for *you*! The things I am teaching you here are meant to be questions and meant to be practiced. The more you practice the more comfortable you will become, and the more likely you will not suffer angst at what financial challenges will come your way. Trust me, there will be plenty of other things you will encounter that should attract your attention. Finances are a means, not an ends. They shouldn't dominate your life, but you will need to pay attention to them, not unlike brushing your teeth for a healthy mouth well into your golden years. There may be a topic I have addressed that is of particular interest to you. If that is the case, then research that aspect. No longer are the folios of knowledge housed in a single building; they are widely available on the internet. While you must be wary of some of the information you find on the internet, it houses information from a whole lot of people, like me, who have been willing to comb through the wisdom of many others in order to make books like this possible. Just don't think you have to pay a lot of money to make a lot of money. Money does beget money. That saying is true, but having to pay a lot to make your money go further or paying someone else to manage your money is just not as necessary as it once was. You have the tools to keep your finances as health as your gums. Be strong, and be willing to learn to make your own financial situation what you want it to be.

www.ingramcontent.com/pod-product-compliance
Lightning Source LLC
Chambersburg PA
CBHW030704220526
45463CB00005B/1903